Praise for

INFORMED INTERCESSION

George Otis, Jr. makes a clear, compelling case that spiritual mapping can accelerate the Church's ability to impact a city for Christ. This book is a must-read for pastors, evangelists, intercessors, lay leaders and prayer warriors who would see their city changed by the gospel of Jesus Christ.

JIM HERRINGTON
City Facilitator, Mission Houston
Houston, Texas

George Otis, Jr., is a pioneer in extending God's kingdom through informed, strategic intercessory prayer. *Informed Intercession* is undeniably one of the great tools for churches worldwide to use in unlocking the spiritual doors to their communities and release the blessings of God. This book is one of a kind.

FRANK DAMAZIO
Senior Pastor, City Bible Church
Portland, Oregon

This book has become the definitive living scale for us in Japan to assure our steps to revival. We now look forward to sweeping transformation with great expectation.

PAUL K. ARIGA
President, All Japan Revival Mission

This book will shake the foundations of the intercessory prayer movement. Here for the first time, we have a comprehensive exploration of spiritual mapping and how such a tool aids intercessors in tranforming a community for Christ.

DUTCH SHEETS
Author of *Intercessory Prayer*
Colorado Springs, Colorado

Once again, George Otis, Jr. has produced an effective guideline for ministries that want to change the destiny of their nation. The Church has entered an unparalleled phase of maturity. Leaders who harness this maturity by putting the principles of this book into practice will make a lasting impact for the kingdom of God.

HAROLD CABALLEROS
Pastor, El Shaddai Church
Guatemala City, Guatemala

If you read only one book on spiritual mapping, *Informed Intercession* should be it! Informative, practical and inspiring, the principles in this book are instrumental in praying targeted prayers that will transform your city.

CINDY JACOBS
Cofounder, Generals of Intercession
Colorado Springs, Colorado

Insightful, challenging and stretching are all appropriate—but inadequate—words to describe this remarkable book. I believe that every pastor, church leader and individual Christian who is committed to the fulfillment of the Great Commission will be challenged and motivated as they prayerfully consider the profound and practical insights shared by George Otis, Jr.

PAUL A. CEDAR
Chairman, Mission America
Palm Desert, California

In eighteen cities on five continents, George Otis, Jr. has seen what so many of us long for—communities transformed by the power and presence of God. Throughout this book the author describes the undeniable signs of God's transforming presence in a city. But he is more than a reporter of observable facts; he focuses attention on the unseen spiritual factors that can prevent—or lead to—community transformation. His question is a simple one: Why are things as they are and what must be done in heaven and on earth to change them? The answer will change your life and your city! *Informed Intercession* is a tool kit of spiritual diagnostics that will lead intercessors into greater fervency and focus. You can be sure the twenty-first-century Church will fight with far greater spiritual effectiveness because of George Otis, Jr.

JACK DENNISON
Dawn Ministries
Colorado Springs, Colorado

Informed
Intercession

GEORGE OTIS, JR.

Renew
FROM GOSPEL LIGHT
A DIVISION OF GOSPEL LIGHT
VENTURA, CALIFORNIA, U.S.A.

Published by Renew Books
A Division of Gospel Light
Ventura, California, U.S.A.
Printed in U.S.A.

Renew Books is a ministry of Gospel Light, an evangelical Christian publisher
dedicated to serving the local church. We believe God's vision for Gospel Light
is to provide church leaders with biblical, user-friendly materials that will help
them evangelize, disciple and minister to children, youth and families.

It is our prayer that this Renew book will help you discover biblical truth for
your own life and help you meet the needs of others. May God richly bless you.

*For a free catalog of resources from Renew Books/Gospel Light please contact your
Christian supplier or contact us at* 1-800-4-GOSPEL *or at* www.gospellight.com.

Cover Design by Kevin Keller
Interior Design by Debi Thayer
Edited by William Simon

Library of Congress Cataloging-in-Publication Data
　　Otis, George, Jr. 1953-
　　Informed intercession / George Otis, Jr.
　　　　p.　　　cm.
　　Includes bibliographical references.
　　ISBN 0-8307-1937-7
　　1. Intercessory prayer—Christianity.　　　2. Community—Religious
　　aspects—Christianity.　　3 Spiritual warfare.　　　I. Title.
　　BV210.2.085　1999
　　269'.2—dc21　　　　　　99-13577　　　　　　　　　CIP

　　4　5　6　7　8　9　10　11　12　/　05　04　03　02　01　00

Rights for publishing this book in other languages are contracted by Gospel
Literature International (GLINT). GLINT also provides technical help for the
adaptation, translation and publishing of Bible study resources and books in
scores of languages worldwide. For further information, write to GLINT, P.O.
Box 4060, Ontario, CA 91761-1003, U.S.A. You may also send E-mail to
Glintint@aol.com or visit their website at www.glint.org.

CONTENTS

FOREWORD

The most significant new development for Christian leaders that has surfaced in the 1990s is that God's people are now positioned to complete the Great Commission of Jesus in the life span of this present generation. No previous generation could have said this, one reason being that no previous generation has had the technological tools to measure the precise dimensions of the remaining task.

I have enjoyed the remarkable privilege throughout this decade of being in a place from which I could observe firsthand many of the significant ways that God has been equipping His people for this special hour. One of the most comforting facts for a person in my senior citizen cohort is that God has been raising up such an extraordinary group of leaders for His kingdom in the generation following mine. At the risk of seeming to slight others who would also fit well into this list, I think of some of my closer associates such as John Dawson, Cindy Jacobs, Ed Silvoso, Bob Beckett, Ted Haggard, Alice and Eddie Smith, John Robb, David Cannistraci, and in particular the author of this book, George Otis, Jr. I can say with great confidence that the Body of Christ is in good hands for the future.

Through these and many others like them, the Holy Spirit has been speaking some new things to the churches. They have the "ear to hear" that Jesus spoke about in His letters to the churches in Revelation. These things, of course, are not new to God. They are scriptural, and indeed, a few members of the Body of Christ were tuned in to them long before the rest of us began to catch on. But it seems that this is the decade in which God has chosen to entrust these powerful spiritual principles to leaders in various Christian traditions so that we can all participate to the maximum in making disciples in all the remaining unreached nations or people groups.

At the beginning of the decade, many of us began talking to each other about strategic-level spiritual warfare, confronting the higher-ranking principalities and powers assigned to keep people groups or countries or cites or neighborhoods or other territories in spiritual darkness. The question soon arose as to whether it was possible, and if so to what extent it might be feasible, to identify these powers and learn how they operate. This brought spiritual mapping to the surface. Through spiritual mapping it soon became clear that some of the strongholds that the enemy was using were deeply rooted in the actions of past generations. What, if anything, could be done about this? A significant part of the answer to that question came as the concepts surrounding identificational repentance began to be explored around mid-decade. As we in repentance began to ask God to "heal the land" (2 Chron. 7:14), we then began to realize how little we knew about stewardship of the land and about the increased spiritual authority that is released when leaders become sincerely committed to the geographical sphere to which they have been assigned.

That sums up in a few words the major advances of the past few years in spiritual weaponry. Central to all of them is the subject of this book, *Informed Intercession: Transforming Your Community Through Spiritual Mapping and Strategic Prayer.* The title reflects a basic premise with which I fully agree: Accurately informed intercession is a critical component in transforming entire communities for Christ. We all know and practice this principle when, for example, we pray for a friend. If they ask for prayer, our first question is, "What do you want me to pray for?" and we go on from there. But only recently have we learned how to ask such questions to our community and get the answers we need. George Otis, Jr., has been the pioneer of this important discipline that we now call "spiritual mapping."

As might be expected, the novelty of an activity such as spiritual mapping attracts its share of flakes. While they may be somewhat of an embarrassment to the rest of us, I do admire their zeal. Furthermore, as I have tracked some of them down and discussed this with them, I have yet to meet one who wants to be a flake. They will be the first to admit that they would love to have more role models and better instruction.

The book you have in your hands will meet those needs. This is a remarkable document that will raise the whole spiritual mapping movement to new levels of integrity and usefulness. I would hate to try to use a bread machine or a computer or a chain saw for the first time without an operator's manual. I am grateful that we now have the operator's manual for those who desire to attempt spiritual mapping.

What is spiritual mapping for? This can easily become so fascinating that it seems to be an end in itself. George Otis will have nothing of that! The goal is not just to gather information for the sake of deeper knowledge of the devices of Satan. The goal is nothing less than community transformation. Is this a high standard? It certainly is, and as you read this book you will be increasingly grateful, as I was, for the demands for excellence which persist from beginning to end. For those of us who deeply desire to serve and please the Lord of lords, nothing else would be acceptable.

C. Peter Wagner
Fuller Theological Seminary

PREFACE

WELCOME TO THE FRONT LINES OF SPIRITUAL WARFARE!

The guide you now hold in your hands is part of a new generation of practical resources that have been developed for today's serious-minded intercessors and evangelists. Whatever your ultimate ministry assignment might be, it is my hope—and conviction—that these pages will prove to be of great practical benefit.

For nearly 10 years now, The Sentinel Group has broken new ground in the fields of spiritual mapping and community transformation. Under the direction of the Holy Spirit we have expanded the modern spiritual warfare dictionary and taught thousands of international Christians to discern the social and spiritual dynamics at work in their neighborhoods. And we have done it with an emphasis on spiritual balance and measurable results.

This is not ultimately a book about ideas. While there is nothing inherently wrong with ideas, today's Christian marketplace is inundated with notions that are untagged and untested. It is cluttered with sudden brainstorms and adapted theories. What we need, however, are historical accounts, real world examples of God's handiwork. And that is what we offer you. The information contained in the following pages derives from Sentinel's decade-long examination of actual case studies—both biblical and contemporary. Familiarize yourself with these success stories and you will discern important principles and patterns. Apply these principles and your town will be added to the growing list of divinely transformed communities.

WHY THIS GUIDE WAS CREATED

Over the last several years, interest in prayer and spiritual warfare has exploded. Across North America, and indeed throughout the world, hundreds of local churches, mission agencies and prayer fellowships have discovered afresh the awesome power of focused intercession.

Along with this renewed interest in prayer has come a growing demand for tools that will allow believers to sustain fervent intercession. The discipline of spiritual mapping, which escalates fervor by enhancing vision, fits the bill perfectly.

Armed with interesting research questions and case studies, thousands of spiritual mapping projects have sprung up recently in communities throughout the world. Most of these initiatives have been pursued with genuine care and resolve, although questionable motives and sloppy methodologies have disabled many others.

Other campaigns have fallen prey to individualization. Data acquisition methodologies, analytical standards and report layouts resemble a basket of mixed fruit. For this reason, the current body of spiritual mapping research does not easily lend itself to comparative analysis.

Recognizing this problem, The Sentinel Group has developed a standardized approach to spiritual mapping that allows for both coherence and customization. This approach, which is laid out in the following chapters, has been fully field-tested and is easy to learn and maintain. Additional help, if it is needed, is available through videos, seminars and on-line services (see appendix 4).

It is time to repair the broken altars of your community so the fire of heaven can come down. It is time to prepare for a visitation of the Holy Spirit.

George Otis, Jr.
Lynnwood, WA
January 1999

~≈~

SNAPSHOTS OF GLORY

For some time now, we have been hearing reports of large-scale conversions in places like China, Argentina and Nepal. In many instances, these conversions have been attended by widespread healings, dreams and deliverances. Confronted with these demonstrations of divine power and concern, thousands of men and women have elected to embrace the truth of the gospel. In a growing number of towns and cities, God's house is suddenly the place to be.

In some communities throughout the world, this rapid church growth has also led to dramatic sociopolitical transformation. Depressed economies, high crime rates and corrupt political structures are being replaced by institutional integrity, safe streets and financial prosperity. Impressed by the handiwork of the Holy Spirit, secular news agencies have begun to trumpet these stories in front-page articles and on prime-time newscasts.

If these transformed communities are not yet common, they are certainly growing in number. At least a dozen case studies have been documented in recent years, and it is likely that others have gone unreported. Of those on file, most are located in Africa and the Americas. The size of these changed communities ranges from about 15,000 inhabitants to nearly 2 million.

Given the extent of these extraordinary stories—and keeping in mind the function of this handbook—I have limited my reporting to select highlights. Despite their brevity, these abridged accounts nevertheless offer glorious "snapshots" of the Holy Spirit at work in our day. Readers interested in more details can find them in books like *Commitment to Conquer* (Bob Beckett, Chosen Books, 1997), *The Twilight Labyrinth* (George Otis, Jr., Chosen Books, 1997) and *Praying with Power* (C. Peter Wagner, Regal Books, 1997).

MIRACLE IN MIZORAM

One of the earliest and largest transformed communities of the twentieth century is found in Mizoram, a mountainous state in northeastern India. The region's name translates as "The Land of the Highlanders." It is an apt description as a majority of the local inhabitants, known as Mizos, live in villages surrounded by timbered mountains and scenic gorges.

The flora is not entirely alpine, however, and it is not uncommon to see hills covered with bamboo, wild bananas and orchids. The Mizos are hearty agriculturists who manage to grow ample crops of rice, corn, tapioca, ginger, mustard, sugar cane, sesame and potatoes.

But it is not farming prowess that sets Mizoram's 750,000 citizens apart. Nor, for that matter, is it their Mongol stock. Rather it is the astonishing size of the national church, estimated to be between 80 and 95 percent of the current population. This achievement is all the more remarkable in view of the fact that Mizoram is sandwiched precariously between Islamic Bangladesh to the west, Buddhist Myanmar to the east and south, and the Hindu states of Assam, Manipur and Tripura to the north.

Before the arrival of Christian missionaries in the late nineteenth century, local tribes believed in a spirit called Pathan. They also liked to remove the heads of their enemies. But in just four generations Mizoram has gone from being a fierce head-hunting society to a model community—and quite possibly the most thoroughly Christian place of comparable size on earth. Certainly in India there is no other city or state that could lay claim to having no homeless people, no beggars, no starvation and 100 percent literacy.

The churches of Mizoram currently send 1,000 missionaries to surrounding regions of India and elsewhere throughout the world. Funds for this mission outreach are generated primarily through the sale of rice and firewood donated by the believers.

Every time a Mizo woman cooks rice, she places a handful in a special "missionary bowl." This rice is then taken to the local church, where it is collected and sold at the market.

Even the non-Christian media of India have recognized Christianity as the source of Mizoram's dramatic social transformation. In 1994 Mizoram celebrated its one-hundredth year of contact with Christianity, which began with the arrival of two missionaries, William Frederick Savage and J. H. Lorraine. On the occasion of this centennial celebration, *The Telegraph* of Calcutta (February 4, 1994) declared:

> Christianity's most reaching influence was the spread of education... Christianity gave the religious a written language and left a mark on art, music, poetry, and literature. A missionary was also responsible for the abolition of traditional slavery. It would not be too much to say that Christianity was the harbinger of modernity to a Mizo society.

A less quantifiable but no less palpable testimony to the Christian transformation of Mizoram is the transparent joy and warmth of the Mizo people. Visitors cannot fail to observe "the laughing eyes and smiling faces," in the words of one reporter, on the faces of the children and other residents of Mizoram. And nowhere is this spirit of divine joy more evident than in the churches, where the Mizo's traditional love of music and dance has been incorporated into worship. The generosity of the people is also seen in their communal efforts to rebuild neighbors' bamboo huts destroyed by the annual monsoons.

Eighty percent of the population of Mizoram attends church at least once a week. Congregations are so plentiful in Mizoram that, from one vantage point in the city of Izol, it is possible to count 37 churches. Most fellowships have three services on Sunday and another on Wednesday evening.[1]

The state of Mizoram is governed by a 40-member assembly that convenes in the capital of Aizawl. Although there are different political parties, all of them agree on the ethical demands of political office in Mizoram. Specifically, all candidates must be:

- persons with a good reputation
- diligent and honest
- clean and uncorrupt
- nondrinkers
- morally and sexually unblemished
- loyal to the law of the land
- fervent workers for the welfare of the people
- loyal to their own church

How many of our political leaders could pass this test? For that matter, how many of our religious leaders could pass?

ALMOLONGA, GUATEMALA

In the mid-1970s, the town of Almolonga was typical of many Mayan highland communities: idolatrous, inebriated and economically depressed. Burdened by fear and poverty, the people sought support in alcohol and a local idol named Maximon. Determined to fight back, a group of local intercessors got busy, crying out to God during evening prayer vigils. As a consequence of their partnership with the Holy Spirit, Almolonga, like Mizoram, has become one of the most thoroughly transformed communities in the world. Fully 90 percent of the town's citizens now consider themselves to be evangelical Christians. As they have repudiated ancient pacts with Mayan and syncretistic gods, their economy has begun to blossom. Churches are now the dominant feature of Almolonga's landscape and many public establishments boast of the town's new allegiance.

Almolonga is located in a volcanic valley about 15 minutes

west of the provincial capital of Quetzaltenango (Xela). The town meanders for several kilometers along the main road to the Pacific coast. Tidy agricultural fields extend up the hillsides behind plaster and cement block buildings painted in vivid turquoise, mustard and burnt red. Most have corrugated tin roofs, although a few, waiting for a second story, sprout bare rebar. The town's brightly garbed citizens share the narrow streets with burros, piglets and more than a few stray dogs.

Although many Christian visitors comment on Almolonga's "clean" spiritual atmosphere, this is a relatively recent development. "Just twenty years ago," reports Guatemala City pastor Harold Caballeros, "the town suffered from poverty, violence and ignorance. In the mornings you would encounter many men just lying on the streets, totally drunk from the night before. And of course this drinking brought along other serious problems like domestic violence and poverty. It was a vicious cycle."

Donato Santiago, the town's aging chief of police, told me during an October 1998 interview that he and a dozen deputies patrolled the streets regularly because of escalating violence. "People were always fighting," he said. "We never had any rest." The town, despite its small population, had to build four jails to contain the worst offenders. "They were always full," Santiago remembers. "We often had to bus overflow prisoners to Quetzaltenango." There was disrespect toward women and neglect of the family. Dr. Mell Winger, who has also visited Almolonga on several occasions, talked to children who said their fathers would go out drinking for weeks at a time. "I talked to one woman," Winger recalls, "whose husband would explode if he didn't like the meal. She would often be beaten and kicked out of the home."

Pastor Mariano Riscajché, one of the key leaders of Almolonga's spiritual turnaround, has similar memories. "I was raised in misery. My father sometimes drank for forty to fifty consecutive days. We never had a big meal, only a little tortilla with a small glass of coffee. My parents spent what little money they had on alcohol."

In an effort to ease their misery, many townspeople made pacts with local deities like Maximon (a wooden idol rechristened San Simon by Catholic syncretists), and the patron of death, Pascual Bailón. The latter, according to Riscajché, "is a spirit of death whose skeletal image was once housed in a chapel behind the Catholic church. Many people went to him when they wanted to kill someone through witchcraft." The equally potent Maximon controlled people through money and alcohol. "He's not just a wooden mask," Riscajché insists, "but a powerful spiritual strongman." The deities were supported by well-financed priesthoods known as confradías.[2]

During these dark days the gospel did not fare well. Outside evangelists were commonly chased away with sticks or rocks, while small local house churches were similarly stoned. On one occasion six men shoved a gun barrel down the throat of Mariano Riscajché. As they proceeded to pull the trigger, he silently petitioned the Lord for protection. When the hammer fell, there was no action. A second click. Still no discharge.

In August 1974 Riscajché led a small group of believers into a series of prayer vigils that lasted from 7 P.M. to midnight. Although prayer dominated the meetings, these vanguard intercessors also took time to speak declarations of freedom over the town. Riscajché remembers that God filled them with faith. "We started praying, 'Lord, it's not possible that we could be so insignificant when your Word says we are heads and not tails.'"

In the months that followed, the power of God delivered many men possessed by demons associated with Maximon and Pascual Bailón. Among the more notable of these was a Maximon cult leader named José Albino Tazej. Stripped of their power and customers, the confradías of Maximon made a decision to remove the sanctuary of Maximon to the city of Zunil.

At this same time, God was healing many desperately diseased people. Some of these healings led many to commit their lives to Christ (including that of Mariano's sister-in-law Teresa, who was actually raised from the dead after succumbing to complications associated with a botched cesarean section).

This wave of conversions has continued to this day. By late 1998 there were nearly two dozen evangelical churches in this Mayan town of 19,000, and at least three or four of them had more than 1,000 members. Mariano Riscajché's El Calvario Church seats 1,200 and is nearly always packed. Church leaders include several men who, in earlier years, were notorious for stoning believers.

Nor has the move of God in Almolonga been limited to church growth. Take a walk through the town's commercial district and you will encounter ubiquitous evidence of transformed lives and social institutions. On one street you can visit a drugstore called "The Blessing of the Lord." On another you can shop at "The Angels" store. Feeling hungry? Just zip into "Paradise Chicken," "Jireh" bakery or the "Vineyard of the Lord" beverage kiosk. Need building advice? Check out "Little Israel Hardware" or "El Shaddai" metal fabrication. Feet hurt from shopping? Just take them to the "Jordan" mineral baths for a good soak.

If foreigners find this public display of faith extraordinary, Mariano sees it as perfectly natural. "How can you demonstrate you love God if you don't show it? Didn't Paul say, 'I am not ashamed of the gospel'?"

The contents of the stores have also changed. Mell Winger recalls visiting a small *tienda* where the Christian proprietor pointed to a well-stocked food shelf and said, "This was once full of alcohol." Town bars have not fared any better. Harold Caballeros explains: "Once people stopped spending their money on alcohol they actually bought out several distressed taverns and turned them into churches. This happened over and over again." One new bar did open during the revival, but it only lasted a couple of months. The owner was converted and now plays in a Christian band.

As the drinking stopped, so did the violence. For 20 years the town's crime rate has declined steadily. In 1994, the last of Almolonga's four jails was closed. The remodeled building is now called the "Hall of Honor" and is used for municipal ceremonies and weddings. Leaning against the door, police chief Donato Santiago offered a knowing grin. "It's pretty uneventful around here," he said.

Even the town's agricultural base has come to life. For years, crop yields around Almolonga were diminished through a combination of arid land and poor work habits. But as the people have turned to God they have seen a remarkable transformation of their land. "It is a glorious thing," exclaims a beaming Caballeros. "Almolonga's fields have become so fertile they yield three harvests per year." In fact, some farmers I talked to reported their normal 60-day growing cycle on certain vegetables has been cut to 25. Whereas before they would export four truckloads of produce per month, they are now watching as many as 40 loads a day roll out of the valley.

Nicknamed "America's Vegetable Garden," Almolonga's produce is of biblical proportions. Walking through the local exhibition hall I saw (and filmed) five-pound beets, carrots larger than my arm and cabbages the size of oversized basketballs.[3] Noting the dimensions of these vegetables and the town's astounding 1,000 percent increase in agricultural productivity, university researchers from the United States and other foreign countries have beat a steady path to Almolonga.

"Now," says Caballeros, "these brothers have the joy of buying big Mercedes trucks—with cash." And they waste no time in pasting their secret all over the shiny vehicles. Huge metallic stickers and mud flaps read "The Gift of God," "God Is My Stronghold" and "Go Forward in Faith."

Some farmers are now providing employment to others by renting out land and developing fields in other towns. Along with other Christian leaders they also help new converts get out of debt. It is a gesture that deeply impresses Mell Winger. "I think of Paul's words to the Thessalonians when he said, 'We not only gave you the gospel of God but we gave you our own souls as well.' "4

Caballeros agrees: "And that's what these people do. It is a beautiful spectacle to go and see the effect of the gospel, because you can actually see it—and that is what we want for our communities, for our cities and for our nations."

～❧～

BELIEVERS IN ALMOLONGA HAVE NO
INTENTION OF LETTING UP. ON HALLOWEEN DAY
IN 1998, AN ESTIMATED 12,000 TO 15,000 BELIEVERS
GATHERED IN THE MARKET SQUARE TO PRAY.
MANY, UNABLE TO FIND SEATS, HUNG OFF
BALCONIES AND CROWDED CONCRETE STAIRCASES.

～❧～

Despite their success, believers in Almolonga have no intention of letting up. Many fast three times a week and continue to assault the forces of darkness in prayer and evangelism. On Halloween day in 1998, an estimated 12,000 to 15,000 believers gathered in the market square to pray down barriers against the gospel in neighboring towns and around the world.5 Many, unable to find seats, hung off balconies and crowded concrete staircases. Led by the mayor and various Christian dignitaries, they prayed hand in hand for God to take authority over their lives, their town and any hindering spirits.

How significant are these developments? In a 1994 headline article describing the dramatic events in Almolonga, Guatemala's premier newsmagazine *Cronica Semanal* concluded "the Evangelical Church...constitutes the most significant force for religious change in the highlands of Guatemala since the Spanish conquest."6

THE UMUOFAI OF NIGERIA

The Umuofai kindred are spread out in several villages situated near the town of Umuahia in Abia State in southeastern Nigeria.[7] A major rail line links the area with Port Harcourt, about 120 kilometers to the south. Like most parts of coastal Africa, it is distinguished by dense tropical flora and killer humidity.

It is possible, even likely, veteran travelers will not have heard of the Umuofai or their homeland. This is not surprising seeing that the kindred's claim to fame has virtually nothing to do with their size or setting. While their history *does* claim centuries-old roots, the truly newsworthy events are still tender shoots.

Indeed the interesting chapter of the Umuofai story began as recently as 1996. Two Christian brothers, Emeka and Chinedu Nwankpa, had become increasingly distressed over the spiritual condition of their people. While they did not know everything about the Umuofai kindred, or their immediate Ubakala clan, they knew enough to be concerned. Not only were there few Christians, but there was also an almost organic connection with ancestral traditions of sorcery, divination and spirit appeasement. Some even practiced the demonic art of shape-shifting.

Taking the burden before the Lord, the younger brother, Chinedu Nwankpa, was led into a season of spiritual mapping. After conducting a partial 80-day fast, he learned that his primary assignment (which would take the good part of a year) was to spend one day a week with clan elders investigating the roots of prevailing idolatry—including the role of the ancestors and shrines. He would seek to understand how and when the Ubakala clan entered into animistic bondage. According to older brother Emeka, a practicing lawyer and international Bible teacher, this understanding was critical. When I asked why, Emeka responded, "When a people publicly renounce their ties to false gods and philosophies, they make it exceedingly undesirable for the enemy to remain in their community."

The study was finally completed in late 1996. Taking their findings to prayer, the brothers soon felt prompted to invite kindred leaders and other interested parties to attend a special meeting. "What will be our theme?" they asked. The Master's response was quick and direct. "I want you to speak to them about idolatry."

On the day of the meeting, Emeka and Chinedu arrived unsure of what kind of crowd they would face. Would there be five or fifty? Would the people be open or hostile? What they actually encountered stunned them. The meeting place was not only filled with 300 people, but the audience also included several prominent clan leaders and witch doctors. "After I opened in prayer," Emeka recalls, "this young man preaches for exactly 42 minutes. He brings a clear gospel message. He gives a biblical teaching on idolatry and tells the people exactly what it does to a community. When he has finished, he gives a direct altar call. And do you know what happens? Sixty-one adults respond, including people from lines that, for eight generations, had handled the traditional priesthood.

"Let me give you an idea of what I am talking about. There is a local spirit that is supposed to give fertility to the earth. The people of the community believed this particular spirit favored farmers who planted yams—an old uncle to the potato. A male from each generation was dedicated to this spirit to insure his blessing. When this priest was ready to die, he had to be taken outside so that the heavenly alignment could be undone. He was buried in the night with his head covered with a clay pot. Then, a year after the burial, the skull was exhumed and put in the shrine. These skulls and other sacred objects were never allowed to touch the ground. Of course, sacrifices were also made from time to time. This was the way of life in our community for eight generations."

When the minister finished the altar call, the Nwankpa brothers were startled to see a man coming forward with the sacred skull in his hands. Here in front of them was the symbol and receptacle of the clan's ancestral power. "By the time the session ended," Emeka marvels, "eight other spiritual custodians had also come forward. If I had not been there in the flesh, I would not have believed it."

As Emeka was called forward to pray for these individuals, the Holy Spirit descended on the gathering and all the clan leaders were soundly converted. The new converts were then instructed to divide up into individual family units—most were living near the village of Mgbarrakuma—and enter a time of repentance within the family. This took another hour and twenty minutes. During this time people were under deep conviction, many rolling on the ground, weeping. "I had to persuade some of them to get up," Emeka recalls.

After leading this corporate repentance, Emeka heard the Lord say, "It is now time to renounce the covenants made by and for this community over the last 300 years." Following the example of Zechariah 12:10–13:2, the Nwankpas led this second-phase renunciation. "We were just about to get up," Emeka remembers, "and the Lord spoke to me again. I mean He had it all written out. He said, 'It is now time to go and deal with the different shrines.' So I asked the people, 'Now that we have renounced the old ways, what are these shrines doing here?' And without a moment's hesitation they replied, 'We need to get rid of them!'"

Having publicly renounced the covenants their ancestors had made with the powers of darkness, the entire community proceeded to nine village shrines. The three chief priests came out with their walking sticks. It was tradition that they should go first. Nobody else had the authority to take such a drastic action. So the people stood, the young men following the elders and the women remaining behind in the village square. Lowering his glasses, Emeka says, "You cannot appreciate how this affected me personally. Try to understand that I am looking at my own chief. I am looking at generations of men that I have known, people who have not spoken to my father for thirty years, people with all kinds of problems. They are now born-again!"

One of these priests, an elder named Odogwu-ogu, stood before the shrine of a particular spirit called Amadi. He was the oldest living representative of the ancestral priesthood. Suddenly he began to talk to the spirits. He said, "Amadi, I want you to listen carefully to what I am saying. You were there in the village square this morning. You heard what happened." He then made an announcement that Emeka will never forget:

> Listen, Amadi, the people who own the land have arrived to tell you that they have just made a new covenant with the God of heaven. Therefore all the previous covenants you have made with our ancient fathers are now void. The elders told me to take care of you and I have done that all these years. But today I have left you, and so it is time for you to return to wherever you came from. I have also given my life to Jesus Christ, and from now on, my hands and feet are no longer here.[8]

As he does this, he jumps sideways, lifts his hands and shouts, "Hallelujah!"

"With tears in my eyes," Emeka says, reliving the moment, "I stepped up to anoint this shrine and pray. Every token and fetish was taken out. And then we went through eight more shrines, gathering all the sacred objects and piling them high.

"Gathering again back in the square I said, 'Those who have fetishes in your homes, bring them out because God is visiting here today. Don't let Him pass you by.' At this, one of the priests got up and brought out a pot with seven openings. He said to the people, 'There is poison enough to kill everybody here in that little pot. There is a horn of an extinct animal, the bile of a tiger and the venom of a viper mixed together.' He warned the young men, 'Don't touch it. Carry it on a pole because it is usually suspended in the shrine.' This was piled in the square along with all the ancestral skulls." Soon other heads of households brought various ritual objects—including idols, totems and fetishes—for public burning. Many of these items had been handed down over ten generations.

Emeka then read a passage from Jeremiah 10 that judges the spirits associated with these artifacts. Reminding the powers that the people had rejected them, he said, "You spirits that did not make the heavens and the earth in the day of your visitation, it is time for you to leave this place." The people then set the piled objects on fire. They ignited with such speed and intensity that the villagers took it as a sign that God had been waiting for this to happen for many years. When the fire subsided, Emeka and his brother prayed for individual needs and prophetically clothed the priests with new spiritual garments. Altogether the people spent nine hours in intense, strategic-level spiritual warfare.

Emeka recalls that when it was over, "You could feel the atmosphere in the community change. Something beyond revival had broken out." Two young ministers recently filled the traditional Anglican church with about 4,000 youth. And in the middle of the message, demons were reportedly flying out the door! Having renounced old covenants, the Umuofai kindred have made a collective decision that nobody will ever return to animism. "Today," Emeka says, "everybody goes to church. There is also a formal Bible study going on, and the women have a prayer team that my mother conducts. Others gather to pray after completing their communal sweeping."9

In terms of political and economic development, good things have begun to happen but not as dramatically as in Almolonga. Still, there is evidence that God has touched the land here much like He has in the highlands of Guatemala. Shortly after the public repentance, several villagers discovered their plots were permeated with saleable minerals. One of these individuals was Emeka's own mother, a godly woman whose property has turned up deposits of valuable ceramic clay.

HEMET, CALIFORNIA

For years this searing valley in southern California was known as a pastor's graveyard. Riddled with disunity, local churches were either stagnant or in serious decline. In one case, street prostitutes actually transformed a church rooftop into an outdoor bordello. The entire community had, in the words of pastor Bob Beckett, "a kind of a nasty spiritual feeling to it."

When Beckett arrived on the scene in 1974, Hemet had the personality of a sleepy retirement community, a place where people who had served their tour of duty came to live out a life of ease.[10] Having achieved most of their goals, people simply wanted to be left alone. Though a fair number attended church, they had no appetite for anything progressive, much less evangelistic. Spiritually lethargic clergy were content to simply go through the motions.

But things were not all they seemed. Underneath the surface of this laid-back community was a spiritual dark side that was anything but lethargic. "We discovered," said Beckett, "that illegal and occult activity was thriving in our community." It was a rude awakening.

The Hemet Valley was fast becoming a cult haven. "We had the Moonies and Mormons. We had the 'Sheep People,' a cult that claimed Christ but dealt in drugs. The Church of Scientology set up a state-of-the-art multimedia studio called Golden Era, and the Maharishi Mahesh Yogi purchased a property to teach people how to find enlightenment." The latter, according to Beckett, included a 360-acre juvenile facility where students were given instruction in upper-level transcendental meditation. "We're not talking about simply feeling good; we're talking about techniques whereby people can actually leave their bodies."

These discoveries got Beckett to wondering why the Maharishi would purchase property in this relatively obscure valley and why it would be located in proximity to the Scientologists and the spiritually active Soboba Indian reservation. Sensing something sinister might be lurking beneath the town's glazed exterior, Beckett took out a map and started marking locations where there was identifiable spiritual activity.[11] Noticing these marks were clustered in a specific area, he began to ask more probing questions. "I began to wonder," he said, "if there was perhaps a dimension of darkness I had failed to recognize. I didn't realize it at the time, but I was led into what we now call spiritual mapping."

The deeper this rookie pastor looked, the less he liked what he was seeing. It seemed the valley, in addition to hosting a nest of cults, was also a notable center of witchcraft. And unfortunately this was not a new development. Elderly citizens could recollect looking up at the nearby mountains on previous Halloweens and seeing them illumined by dozens of ritual fires. In Hemet and the neighboring community of Idyllwild, it was not uncommon to find the remains of animal sacrifices long before such matters became part of the public discourse.

Nor were cults the only preexisting problem. Neighborhood youth gangs had plagued the Hemet suburb of San Jacinto for more than a century. When pastor Gordon Houston arrived in 1986 the situation was extremely volatile. His church, San Jacinto Assembly, sits on the very street that has long hosted the town's notorious First Street Gang. "These were kids whose dads and grandfathers had preceded them in the gang. The lifestyle had been handed down through the generations."

The danger was so great around the main gang turf that the police refused to go there without substantial backup. "One time I was walking out in front of my church," Gordon recalls. "Three First Street guys came up behind me, while four others closed in from across the street. They moved me to the center of the street and asked, 'Who are you and what are you doing here?' It was a scary scenario.

"We were one of the first school districts that had to implement a school dress code to avoid gang attire. It was a big problem. There were a lot of weapons on campus and kids were being attacked regularly. The gangs were tied into one of the largest drug production centers in Riverside County."

It turns out the sleepy Hemet Valley was also the methamphetamine manufacturing capital of the West Coast. One former cooker I spoke to in June 1998 (we'll call him Sonny) told me the area hosted at least nine major production laboratories. The dry climate, remote location and "friendly" law enforcement combined to make it an ideal setup. "It was quite amazing," Sonny told me. "I actually had law officers transport dope for me in their police cruisers. That's the way it used to be here."

Sonny cooked methamphetamine in Hemet from 1983 to 1991. His minimum quota was 13 pounds every two weeks—an amount capable of supplying more than a quarter of a million people. And there were times when he and his colleagues doubled this production. Most of the deliveries went to Southern California, Arizona or Utah. Often the deadly powder was trucked out of town disguised as 4x8-foot forms of Sheetrock. "It was fascinating to see it done," Sonny remembered. "Even the paper backing was torn off afterward and sold to people in prison."

The spiritual turnaround for Hemet did not come easily. Neither the Becketts nor the Houstons were early Valley enthusiasts. "I just didn't want to be there," Bob recalls with emphasis. "For the first several years, my wife and I had our emotional bags packed all the time. We couldn't wait for the day that God would call us out of this valley."

The Houstons didn't unpack their bags to begin with. When the San Jacinto position first opened up in 1984, they drove into town in the middle of summer. Gordon remembers it being scorching hot that day. "We had our six-month-old baby in a Pinto Runabout with vinyl seats and no air-conditioning. We drove down the street, took one look at the church and said, 'No thank you.' We didn't even stop to put in a resumé."

It would be three years before the Houstons were persuaded to return to the Hemet Valley. "Even then," Gordon says, "we saw it as a chance to gain some experience, build a good resumé, and then look for other opportunities. God, of course, had something else in mind. I remember Him saying, 'I have a plan, and I'll share it with you—*if* you will make a commitment to this place.' And I'll be honest with you. It was still a tough choice."

For a while, Bob Beckett's spiritual mapping had provided certain stimulation. Then, it too reached a dead end. "The flow of information just seemed to dry up," he remembers. "That was when God asked if we would be willing to spend the rest of ours lives in this valley. He couldn't have asked a worse question. How could I spend the rest of my life in a place I didn't love, didn't care for and didn't want to be a part of?"

Yet God persevered and the Becketts eventually surrendered to His will. "As soon as we did this," Bob reports, "the flow of information opened back up. In retrospect I see that God would not allow us to go on learning about the community's spiritual roots unless we were committed to act on our understanding. I now realize it was our commitment to the valley that allowed the Lord to trust us with the information.[12]

"Once we made this pact, Susan and I fell in love with the community. It might sound a little melodramatic, but I actually went out and purchased a cemetery plot. I said, 'Unless Jesus comes back, this is my land. I'm starting and ending my commitment right here.' Well, God saw that and began to dispense powerful revelation. I still had my research, but it was no longer just information. It was information that was important to me. It was information I had purchased; it belonged to me."

One new area of understanding concerned a prayer meeting Bob had called 15 years prior. Unable to interpret his spiritual site map or a recurring dream that depicted a bear hide stretched over the valley, he had asked 12 men to join him in prayer at a mountain cabin in nearby Idyllwild. Around two o'clock in the morning the group experienced a dramatic breakthrough—just not the one they were expecting. Rather than yielding fresh insight into the site map or bear hide, the action stimulated a new spiritual hunger within the community.

Now that the Becketts had covenanted to stay in the community, God started to fill in the gaps of their understanding. He began by leading Bob to a book containing an accurate history of the San Jacinto mountains that border Hemet and of the Cahuilla Nation that are descendants of the region's original inhabitants. "As I read through this book I discovered the native peoples believed the ruling spirit of the region was called Tahquitz. He was thought to be exceedingly powerful, occasionally malevolent, associated with the great bear, and headquartered in the mountains. Putting the book down, I sensed the Lord saying, 'Find Tahquitz on your map!'

⤜≋⤏

COMMUNITY INTERCESSORS BEGAN USING
SPIRITUAL MAPPING TO FOCUS ON ISSUES AND
SELECT MEANINGFUL TARGETS. WITH REAL TARGETS
AND TIMELINES, THEY COULD ACTUALLY WATCH
THE ANSWERS TO THEIR PRAYERS.

⤜≋⤏

"When I did so, I was shocked to find that our prayer meeting 15 years earlier was held in a cabin located at the base of a one-thousand-foot solid rock spire called Tahquitz peak! I also began to understand that the bear hide God had showed me was linked to the spirit of Tahquitz. The fact that it was stretched out over the community was a reminder of the control this centuries-old demonic strongman wielded, a control that was fueled then, and now, by the choices of local inhabitants. At that point I knew God had been leading us."

Bob explained that community intercessors began using spiritual mapping to focus on issues and select meaningful targets. Seeing the challenge helped them become spiritually and mentally engaged. With real targets and timelines they could actually watch the answers to their prayers. They learned that enhanced vision escalates fervor.

When I asked him to compare the situation in Hemet today with the way things used to be, he did not take long to answer. "We are not a perfect community," he said, "but we never will be until the Perfect One comes back. What I can tell you is that the Hemet Valley has changed dramatically."

The facts speak for themselves. Cult membership, once a serious threat, has now sunk to less than 0.3 percent of the population. The Scientologists have yet to be evicted from their perch at the edge of town, but many other groups are long gone. The transcendental meditation training center was literally burned out. Shortly after praying for their removal, a brushfire started in the mountains on the west side of the valley. It burned along the top of the ridge and then arced down like a finger to incinerate the Maharishi's facility. Leaving adjacent properties unsinged, the flames burned back up the mountain and were eventually extinguished.

The drug business, according to Sonny, has dropped by as much as 75 percent. Gone, too, is the official corruption that was once its fellow traveler. "There was a time when you could walk into any police department around here and look at your files or secure an escort for your drug shipment. The people watching your back were wearing badges. Man, has that changed. If you're breaking the law today, the police are out to get ya. And prayer is the biggest reason. The Christians out here took a multimillion-dollar drug operation and made it run off with its tail between its legs."

Gangs are another success story. Not long ago a leader of the First Street Gang burst down the center aisle of Gordon Houston's church (San Jacinto Assembly) during the morning worship service. "I'm in the middle of my message," Gordon laughs, "and here comes this guy, all tattooed up, heading right for the platform. I had no idea what he was thinking. When he gets to the front, he looks up and says, 'I want to get saved right now!' This incident, and this young man, represented the first fruit of what God would do in the gang community. Over the next several weeks, the entire First Street family came to the Lord. After this, word circulated that our church was off limits. 'You don't tag this church with graffiti; you don't mess with it in any way.' Instead, gang members began raking our leaves and repainting walls that had been vandalized." More recently, residents of the violent gang house across from San Jacinto Assembly moved out. Then, as church members watched, they bulldozed the notorious facility.

Nor are gang members the only people getting saved in Hemet Valley. A recent survey revealed that Sunday morning church attendance now stands at about 14 percent—double what it was just a decade ago. During one 18-month stretch, San Jacinto Assembly altar workers saw more than 600 people give their hearts to Christ. Another prayer-oriented church has grown 300 percent in twelve months.

The individual stories are stirring. Sonny, the former drug manufacturer, was apprehended by the Holy Spirit en route to a murder. Driving to meet his intended victim he felt something take control of the steering wheel. He wound up in the parking lot of Bob Beckett's Dwelling Place Church. It was about 8 o'clock in the morning and a men's meeting had just gotten underway. "Before I got out of the car," Sonny says ruefully, "I looked at the silenced pistol laying on the seat. I remember thinking, 'Oh my God, what am I doing.' So I covered it with a blanket and walked into this prayer meeting. As soon as I did that, it was all over. People are praying around me and I hear this man speak out: 'Somebody was about to murder someone today.' Man, my eyeballs just about popped out of my head. But that was the beginning of my journey home. It took a long time, but I've never experienced more joy in my life."

As of the late 1990s, Hemet also boasted a professing mayor, police chief, fire chief and city manager. If this were not impressive enough, Beckett reckons that one could add about 30 percent of the local law enforcement officers and an exceptional number of high school teachers, coaches and principals. In fact, for the past several years nearly 85 percent of all school district staff candidates have been Christians.

The result, says Gordon, is that "Our school district, after being the laughing stock of Southern California, now has one of the lowest drop-out rates in the nation. In just four years we went from a 4.7 drop-out rate to 0.07. Only the hand of God can do that."

And what of the Valley's infamous church infighting? "Now we are a wall of living stones," Beckett declares proudly. "Instead of competing, we are swapping pulpits. You have Baptists in Pentecostal pulpits and vice versa. You have Lutherans with Episcopalians. The Christian community has become a fabric instead of loose yarn."

Houston adds that valley churches are also brought together by quarterly concerts of prayer and citywide prayer revivals where speaking assignments are rotated among area pastors. "Different worship teams lead songs and salvation cards are distributed equally among us. It is a cooperative vision. We are trying to get pastors to understand there is no church big enough, gifted enough, talented enough, anointed enough, financially secure enough, equipped enough, to take a city all by itself. Yes, God will hold me accountable for how I treated my church. But I am also going to be held accountable for how I pastored my city."

One fellowship is so committed to raising the profile of Jesus Christ in the valley that they have pledged into another church's building program. To Bob Beckett it all makes sense. "It's about building people, not building a church. In fact, it is not even a church growth issue, it is a kingdom growth issue. It's about seeing our communities transformed by the power of the Holy Spirit."

CALI, COLOMBIA

For years Colombia has been the world's biggest exporter of cocaine, sending between 700 hundred and 1,000 tons a year to the United States and Europe alone.[13] The Cali cartel, which controlled up to 70 percent of this trade, has been called the largest, richest and most well-organized criminal organization in history.[14] Employing a combination of bribery and threats, it wielded a malignant power that corrupted individuals and institutions alike.[15]

Randy and Marcy MacMillan, copastors of the Communidad Christiana de Fe, have labored in Cali for more than 20 years. At least 10 of these have been spent in the shadow of the city's infamous drug lords.

Marcy inherited the family home of her late father, a former Colombian diplomat. When illicit drug money began pouring into Cali in the 1980s, the Cocaine lords moved into the MacMillan's upscale neighborhood, buying up entire blocks of luxurious haciendas. They modified these properties by installing elaborate underground tunnel systems and huge 30-foot (10-meter) walls to shield them from prying eyes—and stray bullets. Video cameras encased in Plexiglas bubbles scanned the surrounding area continuously. There were also regular patrols with guard dogs.

"These people were paranoid," Randy recalls. "They were exporting 500 million dollars worth of cocaine a month, and it led to constant worries about sabotage and betrayal. They had a lot to lose."

For this reason, the cartel haciendas were appointed like small cities. Within their walls it was possible to find everything from airstrips and helicopter landing pads to indoor bowling alleys and miniature soccer stadiums. Many also contained an array of gift boutiques, nightclubs and restaurants.

Whenever the compound gates swung open, it was to disgorge convoys of shiny black Mercedes automobiles. As they snaked their way through the city's congested streets, all other traffic would pull to the side of the road. Drivers who defied this etiquette did so at their own risk. Many were blocked and summarily shot. As many as 15 people a day were killed in such a manner. "You didn't want to be at the same stoplight with them," Randy summarized.

Having once been blocked in his own neighborhood, Randy remembers the terror. "They drew their weapons and demanded to see our documents. I watched them type the information into a portable computer. Thankfully the only thing we lost was some film. I will always remember the death in their eyes. These are people that kill for a living and like it."

Rosevelt Muriel, director of the city's ministerial alliance, also remembers those days. "It was terrible. If you were riding around in a car and there was a confrontation, you were lucky to escape with your life. I personally saw five people killed in Cali."

Journalists had a particularly difficult time. They were either reporting on human carnage—car bombs were going off like popcorn—or they were becoming targets themselves. Television news anchor Adriana Vivas said that many journalists were killed for denouncing what the Mafia was doing in Colombia and Cali. "Important political decisions were being manipulated by drug money. It touched everything, absolutely everything."

By the early 1990s, Cali had become one of the most thoroughly corrupt cities in the world. Cartel interests controlled virtually every major institution—including banks, businesses, politicians and law enforcement.

Like everything else in Cali, the church was in disarray. Evangelicals were few and did not much care for each other. "In those days," Rosevelt Muriel recalls sadly, "the pastors' association consisted of an old box of files that nobody wanted. Every pastor was working on his own; no one wanted to join together."

When pastor-evangelists Julio and Ruth Ruibal came to Cali in 1978, they were dismayed at the pervasive darkness in the city. "There was no unity between the churches," Ruth explained. Even Julio was put off by his colleagues and pulled out of the already weak ministerial association.

Ruth relates that during a season of fasting the Lord spoke to Julio saying, "You don't have the right to be offended. You need to forgive." So going back to the pastors, one by one, Julio made things right. They could not afford to walk in disunity—not when their city faced such overwhelming challenges.

Randy and Marcy MacMillan were among the first to join the Ruibals in intercession. "We just asked the Lord to show us how to pray," Marcy remembers. And He did. For the next several months they focused on the meager appetite within the church for prayer, unity and holiness. Realizing these are the very things that attract the presence of God, they petitioned the Lord to stimulate a renewed spiritual hunger, especially in the city's ministers.

As their prayers began to take effect, a small group of pastors proposed assembling their congregations for an evening of joint worship and prayer. The idea was to lease the city's civic auditorium, the Coliseo El Pueblo, and spend the night in prayer and repentance. They would solicit God's active participation in their stand against the drug cartels and their unseen spiritual masters.

Roping off most of the seating area, the pastors planned for a few thousand people. And even this, in the minds of many, was overly optimistic. "We heard it all," said Rosevelt Muriel. "People told us, 'It can't be done,' 'No one will come,' 'Pastors won't give their support.' But we decided to move forward and trust God with the results."

When the event was finally held in May 1995, the naysayers and even some of the organizers were dumbfounded. Instead of the expected modest turnout, more than 25,000 people filed into the civic auditorium—nearly half of the city's evangelical population at the time! At one point, Muriel remembers, "The mayor mounted the platform and proclaimed, 'Cali belongs to Jesus Christ.' Well, when we heard those words, we were energized." Giving themselves to intense prayer, the crowd remained until 6 o'clock the next morning. The city's famous all-night prayer vigil—the "vigilia"—had been born.

Forty-eight hours after the event, the daily newspaper, *El Pais*, headlined, "No Homicides!" For the first time in as long as anybody in the city could remember, a 24-hour period had passed without a single person being killed. In a nation cursed with the highest homicide rate in the world, this was a newsworthy development. Corruption also took a major hit when, over the next four months, 900 cartel-linked officers were fired from the metropolitan police force.[16]

"When we saw these things happening," Randy MacMillan exulted, "we had a strong sense that the powers of darkness were headed for a significant defeat."

In the month of June, this sense of anticipation was heightened when several intercessors reported dreams in which angelic forces apprehended leaders of the Cali drug cartel. Many interpreted this as a prophetic sign that the Holy Spirit was about to respond to the most urgent aspect of the church's united appeal.[17] Intercessors were praying, and heaven was listening. The seemingly invincible drug lords were about to meet their match.

"Within six weeks of this vision," MacMillan recalls, "the Colombian government declared all-out war against the drug lords." Sweeping military operations were launched against cartel assets in several parts of the country. The 6,500 elite commandos dispatched to Cali[18] arrived with explicit orders to round up seven individuals suspected as the top leaders of the cartel.

"Cali was buzzing with helicopters," Randy remembers. "The airport was closed and there were police roadblocks at every entry point into the city. You couldn't go anywhere without proving who you were."[19]

Suspicions that the drug lords were consulting spirit mediums were confirmed when the federalés dragnet picked up Jorge Eliecer Rodriguez at the fortune-telling parlor of Madame Marlene Ballesteros, the famous "Pythoness of Cali."[20] By August, only three months after God's word to the intercessors, Colombian authorities had captured all seven targeted cartel leaders—Juan Carlos Armínez, Phanor Arizabalata, Julian Murcillo, Henry Loaiza, Jose Santacruz Londono and founders Gilberto and Miguel Rodriguez.

Clearly stung by these assaults on his power base, the enemy lashed out against the city's intercessors. At the top of his hit list was Pastor Julio Ceasar Ruibal, a man whose disciplined fasting and unwavering faith was seriously eroding his maneuvering room.

On December 13, 1995, Julio rode into the city with his daughter Sarah and a driver. Late for a pastors' meeting at the Presbyterian Church, he motioned to his driver to pull over. "He told us to drop him off," Sarah recounts, "and that was the last time I saw him."

Outside the church, a hit man was waiting in ambush. Drawing a concealed handgun, the assassin pumped two bullets into Julio's brain at point-blank range.

"I was waiting for him to arrive at the meeting," Rosevelt remembers. "At two o'clock in the afternoon I received a phone call. The man said, 'They just killed Julio.' I said, 'What? How can they kill a pastor?' I rushed over, thinking that perhaps he had just been hurt. But when I arrived on the scene, he was motionless. Julio, the noisy one, the active one, the man who just never sat still, was just lying there like a baby."

"The first thing I saw was a pool of crimson blood," Ruth

recalls. "And the verse that came to me was Psalm 116:15: 'Precious in the sight of the Lord is the death of his saints.' Sitting down next to Julio's body, I knew I was on holy ground.

"I had to decide how I was going to deal with this circumstance. One option was to respond in bitterness, not only toward the man that had done this terrible thing, but also toward God. He had, after all, allowed the early removal of my husband, my daughters' father and my church's pastor. Julio would never see his vision for the city fulfilled. My other choice was to yield to the redemptive purposes of the Holy Spirit, to give Him a chance to bring something lasting and wonderful out of the situation. Looking down at Julio I just said, 'Lord, I don't understand Your plan, but it is well with my soul.' "

Julio Ruibal was killed on the sixth day of a fast aimed at strengthening the unity of Cali's fledgling church. He knew that even though progress had been made in this area, it had not gone far enough. He knew that unity is a fragile thing. What he could not have guessed is that the fruit of his fast would be made manifest at his own funeral.

In shock, and struggling to understand God's purposes in this tragedy, 1,500 people gathered at Julio's funeral. They included many pastors that had not spoken to each other in months. When the memorial concluded these men drew aside and said, "Brothers, let us covenant to walk in unity from this day forward. Let Julio's blood be the glue that binds us together in the Holy Spirit."

It worked! Today this covenant of unity has been signed by some 200 pastors and serves as the backbone of the city's high-profile prayer vigils. With Julio's example in their hearts, they have subordinated their own agendas to a larger, common vision for the city.

Emboldened by their spiritual momentum, Cali's church leaders now hold all-night prayer rallies every 90 days. Enthusiasm is so high that these glorious events have been moved to the largest venue in the city, the 55,000-seat Pascual Guerrero soccer stadium.[21] Happily (or unhappily as the case may be), the demand for seats continues to exceed supply.

In 1996 God led many churches to join in a collective spiritual mapping campaign. To gain God's perspective on their city, they began to gather intelligence on specific political, social and spiritual strongholds in each of Cali's 22 administrative zones (a scene reminiscent of the 41 Hebrew clans that once rebuilt the walls of Jerusalem). The results, stitched together like panels on a patchwork quilt, gave the church an unprecedented picture of the powers working in the city. "With this knowledge," Randy explained, "our unified intercession became focused. As we prayed in specific terms, we began to see a dramatic loosening of the enemy's stranglehold on our neighborhoods.

"A few weeks later we used our spiritual mapping intelligence to direct large prayer caravans throughout Cali. Most of the 250 cars established a prayer perimeter around the city, but a few paraded by government offices or the mansions of prominent cartel leaders. My own church focused on the headquarters of the billionaire drug lord, José Santacruz Londono, who had escaped from Bogota's La Picota prison in January.[22] His hacienda was located just four blocks from my home. The next day we heard that he had been killed in a gun fight with national police in Medellín!"[23]

In partnership with the Holy Spirit, Cali's Christians had taken effective control of the city. What made the partnership work are the same things that always attract the presence of the Lord: sanctified hearts, right relationships and fervent intercession. "God began changing the city," according to Ruth Ruibal, "because His people finally came together in prayer."[24]

As the kingdom of God descended upon Cali, a new openness to the gospel could be felt at all levels of society—including the educated and wealthy. One man, Gustavo Jaramillo, a wealthy businessman and former mayor, told me, "It is easy to speak to upper-class people about Jesus. They are respectful and interested." Raul Grajales, another successful Cali businessman, adds that the gospel is now seen as practical rather than religious. As a consequence, he says, "Many high-level people have come to the feet of Jesus."

During my April 1998 visit to Cali, I had the privilege of meeting several prominent converts, including Mario Jinete, a prominent attorney, media personality and motivational speaker. After searching for truth in Freemasonry and various New Age systems, he has finally come home to Christ. Five minutes into our interview Jinete broke down. His body shaking, this brilliant lawyer who had courageously faced down some of the most dangerous and corrupt figures in Latin America sobbed loudly. "I've lost forty years of my life," he cried into a handkerchief. "My desire now is to subordinate my ego, to find my way through the Word of God. I want to yield to Christ's plan for me. I want to serve Him."

Explosive church growth is one of the visible consequences of the open heavens over Cali. Ask pastors to define their strategy and they respond, "We don't have time to plan. We're too busy pulling the nets into the boat." And the numbers are expanding. In early 1998, I visited one fellowship, the Christian Center of Love and Faith, where attendance has risen to nearly 35,000. What is more, their stratospheric growth rate is being fueled entirely by new converts. Despite the facility's cavernous size (it's a former Costco warehouse), they are still forced to hold seven Sunday services. As I watched the huge sanctuary fill up, I blurted the standard Western question: "What is your secret?" Without hesitating, a church staff member pointed to a 24-hour prayer room immediately behind the platform. "That's our secret," he replied.

Many of Cali's other churches are also experiencing robust growth, and denominational affiliation and location have little to do with it. The fishing is good for everybody and it's good all over town. My driver, Carlos Reynoso (not his real name), himself a former drug dealer, put it this way: "There is a hunger for God everywhere. You can see it on the buses, on the streets and in the cafes. Anywhere you go people are ready to talk." Even casual street evangelists are reporting multiple daily conversions—nearly all the result of arbitrary encounters.

Although danger still lurks in this city of 1.9 million, God is now viewed as a viable protector. When Cali police deactivated a large, 174-kilo car bomb in the populous San Nicolás area in November 1996, many noted that the incident came just 24 hours after 55,000 Christians held their third *vigilia*. Even *El Pais* headlined: "Thanks to God, It Didn't Explode."[25]

Cali's prayer warriors were gratified, but far from finished. The following month church officials, disturbed by the growing debauchery associated with the city's *Feria*, a year-end festival accompanied by 10 days of bull fighting and blowout partying, developed plans to hold public worship and evangelism rallies.

"When we approached the city about this," Marcy recalls, "God gave us great favor. The city secretary not only granted us rent-free use of the 22,000-seat velodromo (cycling arena), but he also threw in free advertising, security and sound support. We were stunned!" The only thing the authorities required was that the churches pray for the mayor, the city and the citizens.

Once underway, the street witnessing and rallies brought in a bounty of souls. But an even bigger surprise came during the final service which, according to Marcy, emphasized the Holy Spirit "reigning over" and "raining down upon" the city of Cali. As the crowd sang, it began to sprinkle outside, an exceedingly rare occurrence in the month of December. "Within moments," Marcy recalls, "the city was inundated by torrential tropical rain. It didn't let up for 24 hours; and for the first time in recent memory, *Feria* events had to be canceled!"

On the evening of April 9, 1998, I had the distinct privilege of attending a citywide prayer vigil in Cali's Pascual Guerrero stadium.

It was no small event, even in the eyes of the secular media. For days leading up to the *vigilia*, local newspapers had been filled with stories linking it to the profound changes that had settled over the community. Evening newscasters looked straight into the camera and urged viewers, whatever their faith, to attend the all-night event.

Arriving at the stadium 90 minutes early, I found it was already a full house. I could feel my hair stand on end as I walked onto the infield to tape a report for CBN News. In the stands, 50,000 exuberant worshipers stood ready to catch the Holy Spirit's fire. An additional 15,000 "latecomers" were turned away at the coliseum gate. Undaunted, they formed an impromptu praise march that circled the stadium for hours.

Worship teams from various churches were stationed at 15-meter intervals around the running track. Dancers dressed in beautiful white and purple outfits interpreted the music with graceful motions accentuated by banners, tambourines and sleeve streamers. Both they and their city had been delivered of a great burden. In such circumstances one does not celebrate like a Presbyterian, a Baptist or a Pentecostal; one celebrates like a person who has been liberated!

Judging from the energy circulating in the stands, I was sure the celebrants had no intention of selling their emancipation short. They were not here to cheer a championship soccer team or to absorb the wit and wisdom of a big-name Christian speaker. Their sole objective on this particular evening was to offer up heartfelt worship and ask God to continue the marvelous work He had been undertaking in their city for 36 consecutive months.

"What you're seeing tonight in this stadium is a miracle," declared visiting Bogota pastor Colin Crawford. "A few years ago it would have been impossible for Evangelicals to gather like this." Indeed, this city that has long carried a reputation as an exporter of death is now looked upon as a model of community transformation. It has moved into the business of exporting hope.

High up in the stadium press booth somebody grabbed my

arm. Nodding in the direction of a casually dressed man at the broadcast counter he whispered, "That man is the most famous sports announcer in Columbia. He does all the big soccer championships." Securing a quick introduction, I learned that Rafael Araújo Gámez is also a newborn Christian. As he looked out over the fervent crowd, I asked if he had ever seen anything comparable in this stadium. Like Mario, he began to weep. "Never," he said with a trembling chin. "Not ever."

At 2:30 in the morning my cameraman and I headed for the stadium tunnel to catch a ride to the airport. It was a tentative departure. At the front gate crowds still trying to get in looked at us like we were crazy. I could almost read their minds. *Where are you going? Why are you leaving the presence of God?* They were tough questions to answer.

As we prepared to enter our vehicle a roar rose up from the stadium. Listening closely, we could hear the people chanting, in English, *"Lift Jesus up, lift Jesus up."* The words seemed to echo across the entire city. I had to pinch myself. Wasn't it just 36 months ago that people were calling this place a violent, corrupt hell-hole? A city whose ministerial alliance consisted of a box of files that nobody wanted?

In late 1998, Cali's mayor and city council approached the ministerial alliance, with an offer to manage a citywide campaign to strengthen the family. The offer, which has subsequently been accepted, gives the Christians full operational freedom and no financial obligation. The government has agreed to open the soccer stadium, sports arena and velodrome to any seminar or prayer event that will minister to broken families.

GLOBAL PHENOMENON

As remarkable as the preceding accounts are, they represent but a fraction of the case studies that could be presented. Several others are worth mentioning in brief.

Topping this list is Kiambu, Kenya, one-time ministry grave-yard located 14 kilometers northwest of Nairobi. In the late 1980s, after years of profligate alcohol abuse, untamed violence and grinding poverty, the Spirit of the Lord was summoned to Kiambu by a handful of intercessors operating out of a grocery store basement known as the "Kiambu Prayer Cave."

According to Kenyan pastor Thomas Muthee, the real break-through came when believers won a highprofile power encounter with a local witch named Mama Jane. Whereas people used to be afraid to go out at night, they now enjoy one of the lowest crime rates in the country. Rape and murder are virtually unheard of. The economy has also started to grow. And new buildings are sprouting up all over town.

In February, pastor Muthee celebrated their ninth anniversary in Kiambu. Through research and spiritual warfare, they have seen their church grow to 5,000 members—a remarkable development in a city that had never before seen a congregation of more than 90 people. And other community fellowships are growing as well. "There is no doubt," Thomas declares, "that prayer broke the power of witchcraft over this city. Everyone in the community now has a high respect for us. They know that God's power chased Mama Jane from town."[26]

The city of Vitória da Conquiste (Victory of the Conquiste) in Brazil's Bahia state, has likewise, experienced a powerful move of God since the mid 1990s. As with other transformed communi-ties, the recovery is largely from extreme poverty, violence and corruption.

Vitória da Conquiste was also a place where pastors spent more pulpit time demeaning their ministerial colleagues than preaching the Word. Desperate to see a breakthrough, local inter-cessors went to prayer. Within a matter of weeks conviction fell upon the church leaders. In late 1996 they gathered to wash one another's feet in a spirit of repentance. When they approached the community's senior pastor—a man who had been among the most critical—he refused to allow his colleagues to wash his feet. Saying he was not worthy of such treatment, he instead lay prostrate on the ground and invited the others to place the soles of their shoes on his body while he begged their forgiveness. Today the pastors of Vitória da Conquiste are united in their desire for a full visitation of the Holy Spirit.[27]

In addition to lifting long-standing spiritual oppression over the city, this action has also led to substantial church growth. Many congregations have recently gone to multiple services. Furthermore, voters in 1997 elected the son of evangelical parents to serve as mayor. Crime has dropped precipitously, and the economy has rebounded on the strength of record coffee exports and significant investments by the Northeast Bank.

Ed Silvoso of Harvest Evangelism International reports similar developments in San Nicolás, Argentina, an economically depressed community that for years saw churches split and pastors die in tragic circumstances. According to Silvoso, this dark mantle came in with a local shrine to the Queen of Heaven that annually attracts 1.5 million pilgrims.

More recently, pastors have repented for the sin of the church and launched prayer walks throughout the community. They have spoken peace over every home, school, business and police station and concentrated intercession over 10 "dark spots" associated with witchcraft, gangs, prostitution and drug addiction. The pastors have also made appointments with leading political, media and religious (Catholic) officials to repent for neglecting and sometimes cursing them.

As a result of these actions the Catholic bishop is preaching Christ and coming to pastors' prayer meetings. The mayor has created a space for pastors to pray in city hall. The local newspaper has printed Christian literature. The radio station has begun to refer call-in problems to a pastoral chaplaincy service. The TV station invites pastors onto live talk shows to pray for the people. In short, the whole climate in San Nicolás has changed.

In other parts of the world God has been at work in *villages* (Navapur, India; Serawak, Malaysia, [Selakau people]; and the North American Arctic) *urban neighborhoods* (Guatemala City; Sao Paulo, Brazil; Resistencia, Argentina; Guayaquil, Ecuador) and even *countries* (Uganda). The United States has witnessed God's special touch in places as far-flung as New York City (Times Square); Modesto, California; and Pensacola, Florida.

Early in my ministry I never thought of investigating transformed communities. I was too preoccupied with other things. In recent days, however, I have become persuaded that something extraordinary is unfolding across the earth. It is, I have come to realize, an expression of the full measure of the kingdom of God. Finding examples of this phenomenon has become my life. And the journey has taken me to the furthest corners of the earth.

This book is about more than stories however. It is also about principles and methodologies. It is about helping others discover the road to community transformation. So read on, friend, and allow the Lord to take you somewhere you have never been—to someplace wonderful.

NOTES

1. Most of the churches are either Baptist or Presbyterian. But there are also Catholic, Seventh Day Adventist, Salvationist and Pentecostal congregations.

2. Although these confradías are no longer welcome in Almolonga, they can still be found in the nearby communities of Zunil and Olintepeque.

3. Almolonga's fields also grow cauliflower, broccoli, radishes, tomatoes, squash, asparagus, leeks and watercress. Their flower market sells gorgeous asters, chrysanthemums and estaditas.

4. See 1 Thessalonians 2:8, *KJV*.

5. Crowd estimates were provided by Mariano Riscajché based on 10,000 plus seats, rotating local believers and the capacity of adjacent buildings. The event was also carried on local cable television.

6. Mario Roberto Morales, "La Quiebra de Maximon," *Cronica Semanal*, June 24-30, 1994, pp. 17,19,20. (In English the headline reads "The Defeat of Maximon.")

7. In African social hierarchy, kindreds are situated between nuclear families and tribes. They can often be spread out in several towns or villages.

8. This is a local expression that means "I have pulled myself out of your clutches."

9. George Otis, Jr., *The Twilight Labyrinth* (Grand Rapids: Chosen Books, 1997), p. 284.

10. Television personality Art Linkletter made the area famous by proposing it as a mobile home center.

11. This action was taken around 1976.

12. Bob believes that community pastors need to be willing to make an openended commitment that only God can close.

13. This is based on estimates developed by the U.S. Drug Enforcement Administration. Colombia is also a major producer of marijuana and heroin. See "Colombia Police Raid Farm, Seize 8 Tons of Pure Cocaine," *Seattle Times*, October 16, 1994, n.p.

14. This statement is attributable to the U.S. Drug Enforcement Agency. See also Pollard, Peter. "Colombia," *Encyclopædia Britannica Online* [database online]. Book of the Year: World Affairs, 1995 [cited March 11, 1997]. Available from www.eb.com/.

15. To keep tabs on their operations, cartel founders Gilberto and Miguel Rodriguez Orejuela installed no fewer than 37 phone lines in their palatial home.

16. Documenting the dimensions of Colombia's national savagery, Bogota's leading newspaper, *El Tiempo*, cited 15,000 murders during the first six months of 1993. This gave Colombia, with a population of 32 million people, the dubious distinction of having the highest homicide rate in the world. See Tom Boswell, "Between Many Fires," *Christian Century*, Vol. III, No. 18, June 1-8, 1994, p. 560.

17. Two years earlier, as a Christmas "gift," the Rodriguez brothers had provided the Cali police with 120 motorcycles and vans.

18. Otis, Jr., *The Twilight Labyrinth*, p. 300.

19. Ibid.
This unique group was comprised of Colombian police, army personnel and *contra* guerrillas. Note: The June 1995 campaign also included systematic neighborhood searches. To insure maximum surprise, the unannounced raids would typically occur at four A.M. "Altogether," MacMillan reported, "The cartel owned about 12,000 properties in the city. These included apartment buildings they had constructed with drug profits. The first two floors would often have occupied flats and security guards to make them look normal, while higher-level rooms were filled with rare art, gold and other valuables. Some of the apartment rooms were filled with stacks of 100-dollar bills that had been wrapped in plastic bags and covered with mothballs. Hot off American streets, this money was waiting to be counted, deposited or shipped out of the country."
The authorities also found underground vaults in the fields behind some of the big haciendas. Lifting up concrete blocks, they discovered stairwells descending into secret rooms that contained up to 9 million dollars in cash. This was so-called "throwaway" money. Serious funds were laundered through banks or pumped into "legitimate" businesses. To facilitate wire transfers, the cartel had purchased a chain of financial institutions in Colombia called the Workers Bank.

20. Dean Latimer, "Cali Cartel Crackdown?" *High Times* [database online]. [Cited 8 August 1995]. Available at www.hightimes.com.

21. The vigils have been held in the Pascual Guerrero stadium since August 1995.

22. After serving six months of his sentence, Santacruz embarrassed officials by riding out of the main gate of the maximum-security prison in a car that resembled one driven by prosecutors.

23. As the authorities probed the mountain of paperwork confiscated during government raids, they discovered at least two additional "capos" of the Cali cartel. The most notorious of these, Helmer "Pacho" Herrera, turned himself in to police at the end of August 1996. The other, Justo Perafán, was not linked to the Cali operations until November 1996 because of a previous connection with the Valle cartel.

24. To appreciate the extent of these changes on the city, one has only to walk past the vacant haciendas of the drug barons. In addition to serving as monuments of human folly, these ghost towns stand as eloquent testimonies of the power of prayer.

25. "Gracias a Dios No Explotó," *El Pais*, Cali, November 6, 1996; "En Cali Desactivan Un 'Carrobomba'," *El Pais*, Cali, November 6, 1996, n.p.

26. For a more complete version of the Kiambu story, see the *Twilight Labyrinth*, pp. 295-298.

27. The pastors came out of this season with a five-part strategy for turning their community around: (1) set aside a day for fasting and confession of sin; (2) require Christian men to improve the way they treat their wives and families; (3) promote reconciliation between churches; (4) raise up trained intercessors for the city; and (5) conduct spiritual mapping.

Chapter 2

THE ROAD TO COMMUNITY TRANSFORMATION

Transformed communities do not materialize spontaneously. If they did we might legitimately wonder why an omnipotent and ostensibly loving God did not turn the trick more often. We would also be left to ponder our own value as intercessors.

Fortunately such thoughts can be banished immediately. This is because community transformation is not an arbitrary event but rather the product of a cause and effect process.

My certainty in this matter derives, first and foremost, from the teachings of Scripture. God's Word makes clear that divine revelation and power are called forth by sanctified hearts, by right relationships and by united, fervent and selfless intercession (see 2 Chron. 7:14; Jer. 29:13; John 15:7; Jas. 5:16; 1 John 3:21,22; 5:14). Colorado Springs pastor Dutch Sheets adds that in the Old Testament era the fire of God was summoned by the presence of an appropriate altar and an acceptable sacrifice (see Exod. 24; Josh. 8:30,31; Judg. 6:17-21; 1 Chron. 21:25,26; Ezek. 43:18-27). To meet this standard it was sometimes necessary to rebuild broken altars and/or tear down false ones (see Judg. 6:25,26; 1 Kings 18:30-38; 2 Kings 23:3-15; Ezra 3:1-6).

In other words, there are definitive steps that we can and should take to position our communities for a visitation of the Holy Spirit. And if the above passages are not reason enough to believe this, you might want to consider recent evidence that shows God's people are acting on this proposition with great success. I know this because I have spent the last several years analyzing more than a dozen newly transformed communities—including those profiled in the previous chapter.

IDENTIFYING COMMON THREADS

Transformation case studies are best considered collectively. A solitary story, no matter how remarkable or inspiring it may be, inevitably comes with a nagging question: Is it reproducible? You are never quite sure.

Bump into this same story ten or twelve times, however, and your confidence will rise. You now have an established pattern, and patterns are compelling. Laden with reproducible principles, patterns transform inspirational stories into potent models.

My own investigation into the factors responsible for transformed communities has yielded several major "hits." These include, but are not limited to, the following five stimuli:

1. Persevering leadership (see Neh. 6:1-16)
2. Fervent, united prayer (see Jon. 3:5-10)
3. Social reconciliation (see Matt. 5:23,24; 18:15-20)
4. Public power encounters (see Acts 9:32-35)
5. Diagnostic research/spiritual mapping (see Josh. 18:8-10)

Although each of these factors recurs often enough to be considered common, two of them—persevering leadership and fervent united prayer—are present in *all* of our transformation case studies. This observation suggests a possible distinction between *core factors* and *contextual factors*. Core factors, given their ubiquity, appear to initiate (or at least signal) divine involvement. Community transformation simply does not occur unless they are present. Contextual factors, on the other hand, are measures commended by God on the basis of local history, habits and ideology.[1] They are the unique and added touch that turns potential into victory.

With this distinction in mind, I want to take a closer look at the two core factors on our list. If they indeed play a central role in community transformation, it seems prudent to become better acquainted with them.

PERSEVERING LEADERSHIP

Determined leaders figure prominently in the scriptural record. Noah spent decades constructing a massive ark while his neighbors mocked him as an eccentric fool. Nehemiah rebuilt the walls of Jerusalem in the face of persistent threats from Sanballat. Jesus ignored protestations from well-meaning friends in order to lay down His life at Calvary.

It should therefore come as no surprise that catalytic leaders associated with recent community transformations have also battled through strong opposition. Exhibiting a characteristic I call *determined activism,* these spiritual-change agents have refused to accept anything less than God's maximum—even when the pressure has come from family members and ministry colleagues.

When things got rough for pastor/evangelist Robert Kayanja during his transformative ministry in a dangerous neighborhood in Kampala, Uganda, his own parents were among those urging him to leave. "God wants to save these people," they said, "but He doesn't want you to die in the process." Christian activists ministering in the city of Cali, Colombia, heard much the same thing. When pastor Julio Caesar Ruibal was gunned down in December 1995, well-meaning friends urged his widow to leave town before the same fate befell her. Ignoring this counsel (and persistent death threats), she became a rallying point for city pastors.

Other warnings have been linked to perceptions about unresponsive attitudes and appropriate ministry venues. In Kenya, when Thomas Muthee announced that that he was planting a church in Kiambu, his ministerial colleagues could only ask, "How will you manage?" One area pastor flatly declared, "The people here don't get saved. We preach, but they don't respond."

Not persuaded by this claim, Thomas went on to found the largest church in Kiambu's history.

Whether we view these determined activists as instruments of divine sovereignty or as magnets for divine intervention, their role is obviously critical to the process of community transformation. In every case their single-minded faith, demonstrated by importunate prayer and a steadfast commitment to the community, led to dramatic results. And while this may strike us as extraordinary, it is has long been the promise and pattern of Scripture.[2]

UNITED PRAYER

The second core factor in community transformation is fervent, united prayer. In each of our featured case studies, breakthroughs occurred when intercessors addressed specific concerns in common cause. Many of these group efforts took on their own unique identities. In Cali, 60,000 intercessors held all-night *vigilias* and circled the city in mobile prayer caravans. In Kampala, hand-holding prayer warriors referred to their daily discipline as the "Wailing Wall." In Kiambu, believers petitioned God from a store basement they dubbed the "Prayer Cave." Their success led to subsequent intercessory campaigns like "Morning Glory" and "Operation Prayer Storm."[3]

In December 1995 Pakistani evangelist Javed Albert established a routine he calls "Tarry Nights" to counter powerful demonic influences associated with shrine pilgrimages and witchcraft activity.[4] These prayer and praise vigils begin at 9:00 P.M. on Thursday and Saturday evenings and continue until dawn. Because participants stand through the entire affair, they are also called "Standers Meetings." The program, which began at Albert's modest church compound in Faisalabad, has since spread to 25 cities and 4,000 people.

United prayer is a declaration to the heavenlies that a community of believers is prepared for divine partnership. When this welcoming intercession is joined by knowledge, it becomes focused—leading to and sustaining the kind of fervent prayer that produces results.

THREE STAGES OF PROGRESS

Recent case studies suggest that the road to community transformation passes through three distinct and measurable stages (see Figure 2.1 below). These include:

1. *Spiritual beachheads,* an initial phase when revived believers enter into united prayer;
2. *Spiritual breakthrough,* a subsequent interval characterized by rapid and substantial church growth;
3. *Spiritual transformation,* a climactic season attended by dramatic socio-political renewal.

The Road to Community Transformation

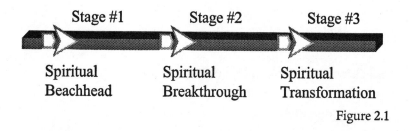

Stage #1	Stage #2	Stage #3
Spiritual Beachhead	Spiritual Breakthrough	Spiritual Transformation

Figure 2.1

A fourth stage called *spiritual maintenance* could easily be added to this list. It is entered whenever liberated communities turn their attention to the business of preserving hard-won victories. For Christian leaders this means continuing to champion the things that attract God's presence: unity, prayer, humility and holiness. For born-again politicians, journalists, businessmen and educators, it means perpetuating Kingdom values through the institutions they serve.

The ideal is that spiritual transformation remains a permanent condition. Unfortunately, history shows that the blossom of revival (to use a loose definition of the term) lasts an average of 36 months.[5] Exceptions exist—the Argentine revival has lingered more than 15 years—but these are few and far between. "Success," in the words of Kenyan pastor Thomas Muthee, "is not where you begin, but where you continue. It is easy to raise your hands. It is hard to keep them up."

My immediate goal, however, is not to discuss the maintenance of transformed communities (this discourse will come in due time) but to examine the process of achieving them. As all true champions have learned, you can only maintain what you have first attained.

We will begin our journey by investigating the role of spiritual beachheads. Do pay attention! More high hopes have been dashed here than any other place on the road to community transformation. It is during this early stage that you must build the spiritual momentum necessary to carry you over the mountains of apathy, pride and unbelief.

ESTABLISHING SPIRITUAL BEACHHEADS

Beachheads are small plots of ground (often a beach) that serve as staging areas for invading military forces. Because of their strategic potential, defending armies will fight vigorously to prevent them from becoming established. As a consequence, most beachheads are secured at high cost.

An example of this exacted price is seen in the opening sequence of Steven Spielberg's acclaimed World War II film *Saving Private Ryan*. As thousands of young GIs hit the beaches at Normandy they are subjected to withering German fire. Most are cut down in the heavy surf, and their bleeding gives new meaning to the term "red tide." A deadly gauntlet of barbed wire, machine guns, land mines and German 88 artillery awaits the "lucky" few that make it onto shore.

When Tom Hanks's character reaches a rallying point behind a protective concrete wall, he turns to a comrade and asks, "Sergeant Horvath, do you know where we are?"

Pausing for a moment, Horvath replies, "Right where we're supposed to be, but nobody else is."

From this wretched, smoking perch, a ragtag band of brave soldiers goes on to establish one of the most famous beachheads in military history. When Spielberg brings the audience back to this hallowed ground a few scenes later, it is cleared of the telltale bodies and barricades. In their place, for as far as the eye can see, is the orderly discharge of hundreds of ships. Even the casual observer cannot mistake the importance of these endless lines of supply. The liberation of Europe has begun.

Beachheads can also be established in the spiritual dimension. Like their counterparts in the material world, these staging areas are the work of warriors—in this case intercessors and evangelists whose ultimate aim is to launch breakthrough assaults on enemy strongholds.

While beachheads can swell quickly with men and material, their initial occupants are few. Some spiritual beachheads have been established by a mere handful of intercessors. The transformation of Hemet, California, began with 12 men praying through the night in a mountain cabin. Robert Kayanja's church-planting effort in the "Beirut of Kampala" started with five prayer warriors. Thomas Muthee established the spiritual beachhead in Kiambu, Kenya, with but a single partner—his wife, Margaret. In each of these cases, inner fears, enemy fire and public apathy thinned dramatically the ranks of hill-taking, camp-making spiritual warriors.

Although this modest level of participation appears to be incompatible with the primary characteristic of spiritual beachheads—namely fervent united prayer—three things must be kept in mind. First, the population of beachheads tends to escalate with time. Breakthrough drives are rarely launched before sufficient troops have accumulated. Second, in some cases even a modest group of intercessors can represent a high percentage of the church. This is especially true in frontier or under-churched areas. Third, united prayer has more to do with heart attitudes than mass movements. As Jesus reminded His disciples in Matthew 18:19,20, God's presence and power is manifest when just two or three believers agree in prayer (see also Eccles. 9:14,15).

If numbers are not essential to successful intercessory beachheads, spiritual passion is. Believers who wish to position their community for spiritual breakthroughs must pour their hearts and souls into the effort. Unless the church is consumed with a burning desire for divine visitation, united prayer will become merely another project.

As I have taught on this subject throughout the world, people often ask me to provide examples of genuine spiritual beachheads. Although inspired by stories of breakthroughs and transformed communities, the results-oriented emphases of these accounts sometimes obscure important formative details.

The good news is that contemporary spiritual beachheads abound—just don't expect uniformity. Depending on their developmental status, they can appear quite different (see Figure 2.2).

Early & Latter-Stage Beachheads

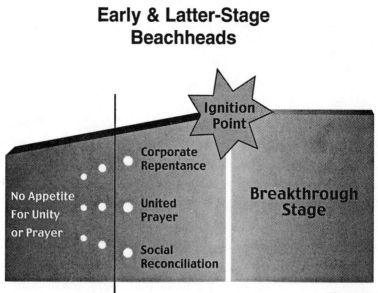

Figure 2.2

Newly formed initiatives are typically small, unpublicized affairs in which a handful of dedicated intercessors seek to stimulate a renewed hunger for unity, holiness and prayer—especially among community pastors. The stakes here are enormous. Without an increased appetite for the things that attract the presence of the Holy Spirit, evangelistic breakthroughs—let alone community transformation—will simply not occur.

Successful beachhead builders are content in their role as supporting actors. They have no craving for the limelight. This characteristic, however, should not be misinterpreted as indifference. Foundational intercessors are also passionate about doing whatever it takes to prepare their communities for divine visitation. Their unceasing petition is that God will replace the Church's bird-like appetite for prayer and unity with a ravenous hunger.

Latter-stage beachheads, by contrast, are nearly always characterized by intense groundswells of corporate repentance, social reconciliation and united prayer. In many instances these developments are sustained by intelligence acquired through cooperative spiritual mapping campaigns.

Given the enormous pent-up energy displayed during latter-stage beachheads, observers have likened this season to a shuddering rocket just prior to launch. Others refer to these exciting days as the "hard labor" that necessarily precedes the birth of a new era.

The bad news is that very few spiritual beachheads ever last long enough to realize their potential as breeding grounds for revival. Most start with good intentions and then fizzle out.

Among the more common reasons for this attrition are weak leadership and the tendency to make unity an end in itself. Pastors gather for prayer but their rendezvous are often lacking in passion. This is because the emphasis is placed on corporate assembly rather than corporate vision. Trying to attract the widest possible cross section of participants, they create an environment in which personal agendas proliferate like mushrooms. In the end, unity is trumped by cordiality. Unable to achieve a common vision, they settle for a common place.

Happily, there are exceptions to this trend. In Oklahoma City, for example, over half of the community's spiritual leaders gather monthly to petition God for a spiritual breakthrough. A principal catalyst for this focused prayer and fasting was the April 1995 bombing of the Murrah Federal Building which claimed 168 lives. In the aftermath of this tragic event the intercessory prayer force in the city jumped from 9 to more than 140 pastors and ministry leaders.

Another important development occurred in September 1996. As the leaders gathered one day for prayer, God revealed to them that their newfound "unity" was still superficial. There was almost no Native American participation—despite the fact Oklahoma hosts more than 60 tribes and the second largest Indian population in the U.S. Deeply convicted, one Anglo believer with deep roots in this state of "soil, oil and toil" repented publicly for the way his ancestors, both in and out of government, had swallowed up land set aside for displaced Native Americans.

The consequences of this Spirit-led action were quick in coming. Welcomed and empowered by this public gesture, Native American attendance at the monthly prayer meetings tripled. Today their voices are heard alongside 1,200 other intercessors that have covenanted to pray for a spiritual breakthrough in the area.

UNITED PRAYER IS NOT ALWAYS UNANIMOUS PRAYER.
A SPIRITUAL CRITICAL MASS CAN BE ACHIEVED EVEN
IF SOME MEMBERS OF THE COMMUNITY CHOOSE
NOT TO PARTICIPATE.

While reconciliation between believers and between the Church and the community is an important catalyst for evangelistic breakthroughs, the history of revival—a term which has been defined so loosely to at various times apply both to spiritual beachheads and spiritual breakthroughs—reveals that general unity is not as critical. Since believers of differing backgrounds and persuasions can and do come together in intercessory common cause over the issues of revival and evangelistic breakthroughs (see Acts 1:14 KJV), unity and united prayer are not necessarily synonymous. In a recent article entitled "Prayer: God's Catalyst for Revival," Robert Bakke wrote:

> [In the 18th century] Count Nicholas Von Zinzendorf gathered an incredibly diverse group of Christians (Catholics, Lutherans, Calvinists, etc.) from across Europe. He was able to forge and sustain their union as a single movement (the Moravians) only when he called his community to a lifestyle of united praying.[6]

It should be pointed out, however, that united prayer is not always unanimous prayer. A spiritual critical mass can be achieved even if some members of the community choose not to participate. This was certainly the case in Charles Finney's day. When the great evangelist launched his ministry in New England over a century ago, many conservative clergy opposed his efforts. Despite this hesitancy, enough intercession was mobilized to usher in the most dramatic season of community transformation in American history.

ACHIEVING SPIRITUAL BREAKTHROUGHS

While united prayer is a potent catalyst for revival, community-wide evangelistic breakthroughs require that intercession be fervent and sustained as well. Like many things that start well, petitions that lose their focus or fervor soon become pipe dreams.

This is not to say that fervent prayer is always articulate. God is a heart reader, not a lip reader (see 2 Chron. 30:18-20; Matt. 6:5-8). When I petitioned God for the life of my two-year-old daughter, who, in 1996, nearly drowned in a swimming pool accident, I did not pause to consider my words. In fact, there was nothing eloquent about my cries and groaning.

At the same time, my prayer *was* fervent. And it was fervent because I was consumed with the details of the case. As I looked down on my daughter's lifeless face, I recognized every tiny crease and curve. I had mapped them over the past two years as I paused to kiss her good night. I was also acquainted with her budding gifts and idiosyncrasies, and I could recall each word spoken over her when she was still in the womb. In short, I prayed hard for this little girl because I knew her (and the situation at hand) intimately.

Community intercession is not much different. To pray fervently for a neighborhood we must first familiarize ourselves with its history and features. And since reality is often painted in shades of gray, this requires us to linger in spaces both dark and light. It is not enough to merely acknowledge the community; we must become acquainted with it—even intimate. True lovers do not refuse to look at their partner's blemishes. Indeed, fervor bred of familiarity.

And perseverance is no less important than fervor. History shows that spiritual breakthroughs are often delayed reactions, their spectacular fireworks the result of an intercessory match struck months, or even years, earlier. The challenge is to keep the fuse burning to the point of ignition.

Two factors have proven particularly effective in sustaining fervent corporate intercession: *progressive revelation* and *positive results*.

In the first instance, people are motivated by new details about the case at hand. The psychology is the same as that which pulls readers through a good mystery novel or hobbyists through a challenging puzzle. In both situations, participants are rewarded with a sense of momentum toward an ultimate solution. Incremental disclosure is not only tolerated, it is enjoyable.

This was certainly the experience of a spiritual mapping team operating out of the El Shaddai Church in Guatemala City, Guatemala, during the early 1990s. Their mission was to identify obstacles to revival in their community. To accomplish this, team members were divided into three working groups that investigated respective historical, physical and spiritual factors.

The process began when God led the historical team to a Mayan archaeological site. As they reviewed the weathered remains, it suddenly became clear that their spiritual challenges were part of an ancient continuum of idolatry and witchcraft. At this precise moment, the physical factors team (which had been operating independently) located a vacant house adjacent to the ruins where occult rituals were being practiced. A third team, comprised of intercessors, received a revelation that the territorial spirit over that place was linked to a human coconspirator whose lifestyle included idolatrous and occult practices.

The next series of developments, which pastor Harold Caballeros describes as "truly exciting," began when the Lord indicated His intention to disclose the man's identity in the city newspaper—even going so far as to reveal the date and page on which the information would appear. When the team finally turned to the appropriate page, they were stunned to find not only the name of the suspect but also a photo matching a precise physical description the Holy Spirit had provided earlier. "To cap it off," writes Caballeros, "we discovered that this man was also the owner of the vacant house where the occult rituals were taking place, right across the street from the archaeological site!"[7]

Where believers are united in their desire to see a community transformed by the power of God, spiritual mapping can provide the kind of revelatory focus that sustains fervent and effectual prayer. When this intelligence is carried into spiritual warfare, God is released to provide an "open door" for ministry (see Col. 4:2-4).[8] Evangelistic breakthroughs and church growth often follow.

Answers to prayer offer equally potent motivation for corporate intercessors. Like progressive revelation, timely results encourage those praying to stick with their assignments. Besides the pleasure associated with seeing desired changes take root in broken communities, there is an exhilaration that comes from knowing our words have moved the Almighty.

To find an example of results sustaining fervent intercession we need look no further than Cali, Colombia. Forty-eight hours after that city's first all-night prayer vigil, the local daily, *El Pais*, reported a notable decrease in homicides. Subsequent intercession targeting corruption and drug trafficking led to the firing of 900 cartel-linked police officers and a roundup of the city's top cocaine bosses.[9]

In recent years both Cali and Guatemala City have experienced *community-wide* church growth, and it is this feature that makes their claims of spiritual breakthrough authentic. Growth that is confined to individual churches, while generally desirable, is not the same thing. This is because there are any number of reasons short of divine visitation that might explain proliferating numbers (including charismatic leadership, quality management and appealing programs). Genuine evangelistic breakthroughs, on the other hand, tend to spread spontaneously across geographic, ethnic and denominational boundaries.

FROM BREAKTHROUGH TO TRANSFORMATION

Given the heady atmosphere that accompanies spiritual breakthroughs, some Christians misinterpret these seasons as the climax of divine activity and intention. This is an understandable, if unfortunate, error. For while spiritual breakthroughs are by definition advanced achievements, they are by no means the end of God's ambitions for a community (see Figure 2.3).

Early Exits

Why Beachheads Fail	Why Breakthroughs End
• Weak Leadership • Tendency to Make Unity an End in itself	• Misinterpreting Breakthroughs as the Climax of Divine Activity. • No Perceived Need for Change.
An emphasis is placed on **corporate assembly** rather than **corporate vision.**	An emphasis is placed on **managed growth** rather than **drastic change.**

Figure 2.3

❧

AS AN INCREASING PERCENTAGE OF THE POPULATION COMES UNDER THE LORDSHIP OF CHRIST, THE SIN-WROUGHT CITADELS OF CORRUPTION, POVERTY, PREJUDICE AND OPPRESSION ARE TRANSFORMED INTO GHOST TOWNS.

❧

If intercessors continue to press in during the spiritual breakthrough phase, a point of critical mass will eventually be reached where community transformation occurs. At this level the social, political and economic fabric of the entire community begins to metamorphose. As an increasing percentage of the population comes under the Lordship of Christ, the sin-wrought citadels of corruption, poverty, violence, prejudice and oppression are transformed into ghost towns. Confirmation of this new heavenly order comes not from Christian triumphalists but from the evening newscasts and banner headlines of the secular media.

This is not to suggest that transformed communities are perfect communities—at least not in a millennial sense. Even sympathetic observers will have little trouble locating blemishes. Violence, immorality and apathy are ubiquitous in our world, and this includes cities that have been visited by divine grace. Spiritual transformation is not a total absence of sin but rather a fresh trajectory with acknowledged fruit. Communities that have been so touched should be measured not by what they still lack but by what they once were.

Asia has arguably experienced more divine visitations than any other region in recent history. This has led to phenomenal church growth in various parts of China, South Korea, India, Bangladesh, Nepal, Indonesia and the Philippines. Less encouraging is the fact that the continent has only one documented case of community transformation—the state of Mizoram in eastern

India (three other cases are currently under investigation). Noting the sharp drop-off between breakthrough and transformation, one cannot help but wonder about the factors responsible for this attrition.

Two reasons stand out. First, as mentioned earlier, there is a tendency for Christians to misinterpret breakthroughs as the climax of divine activity. If people are getting saved and our churches are growing, what more could we ask for? How could these blessed and exciting developments be anything other than God's maximum intent?

The second reason is closely related to the first. Community transformation fails to occur because local inhabitants do not perceive a need for change. Affluent societies in particular tend to be self-sufficient and self-satisfied—qualities that make them poor candidates for divine intervention. They are the collective embodiment of Jesus' teaching about it being "easier for a camel to go through the eye of a needle than for a rich man to enter the kingdom of God" (Matt. 19:24). While the obstacle of affluence (or security) can be overcome, history has shown this to be a rare occurrence.

Of the case studies consulted for this chapter, it is noteworthy that only one—Hemet, California—is located within the industralized world, and even it is faced with significant maintenance challenges. While Asia has long been viewed as distinct from the West, the region's economic growth (recent downturns notwithstanding) has blurred this distinction. Places like Singapore, Japan and Taiwan are now awash in the same abundance and political stability that one finds in Europe and North America. Unfortunately, they have also begun to adopt the self-satisfaction that so often accompanies these blessings.

This problem is compounded in churches with large memberships. When the pastors of these congregations survey their ministries, they see little that would suggest a need for change. Competent staffs are busy running well-conceived programs and the sanctuary is filled every Sunday with a sea of eager faces.

While the status quo is not perfect, neither is it a rationale for extreme measures. Change, if and when it is needed, is best sought in manageable increments.

The danger in this perspective lies in its introversion. Because their sphere of influence is large, the leaders of well-heeled megachurches tend to view their community from inside that circle (see Figure 2.4). They see other churches in the community not as partners in a collective vision but as competitors for market shares. There are exceptions, of course, but not many. The mirror of history reveals that the grander a church or ministry becomes, the more likely it is to succumb to the "Laodicean Syndrome."[10] And one of the primary symptoms of this complex is a subconscious shift from Kingdom mentality to empire mentality.

Smaller churches can also develop empire mentalities of course. But unlike more prosperous ministries, they are often delivered from this condition by persistent reminders of their limitations. Small crowds and tight budgets have a way of commending new approaches and partnerships.

As many churches and communities have discovered, an all-for-one Kingdom mentality is the quickest route to prosperity. In Modesto, California, a new collective vision has led to a citywide harvest of souls numbering in the tens of thousands. Some of the city's fellowships, which come in varying sizes and denominational flavors, have elected to display their singular commitment by replacing old church signboards with new ones that read: THE CHURCH OF MODESTO. Similar scenes have been recorded in Arlington, Texas, and in various cities throughout Latin America.

While many churches today are preoccupied with growing their circle, God's focus is on the area between the circles. He worries not about the one sheep that is found, but the 99 that are lost. He wants to break out of our churches and into local boardrooms, classrooms and courtrooms. In short, He wants to introduce His kingdom into *every* area of society.

Some time ago I took a wrong turn on my way to Sunday

Two Perspectives

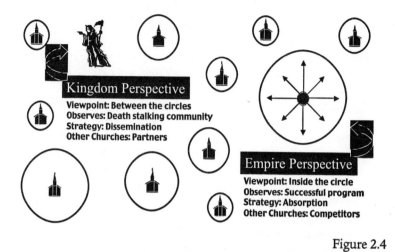

Kingdom Perspective
Viewpoint: Between the circles
Observes: Death stalking community
Strategy: Dissemination
Other Churches: Partners

Empire Perspective
Viewpoint: Inside the circle
Observes: Successful program
Strategy: Absorption
Other Churches: Competitors

Figure 2.4

church services and found myself on unfamiliar streets. This caused me to pay attention to my surroundings in a way I would not have otherwise. The sights on this particular morning disturbed me: a pair of homeless drunks staggering down the sidewalk, a video arcade filled with troubled teens, and hoards of preoccupied antique shoppers.

When I finally pulled into the church parking lot I noticed something else that had escaped me on previous Sundays. An attractive, hand-carved sign advertised "Celebration Services" at 9:00 and 11:00 A.M. On this Sabbath morning, however, I did not feel like celebrating. Whatever blessings I might count clearly did not extend to the streets of my community. I had seen too much.

Most of us want to see things change in our communities. Unfortunately, few of us ever have. We do not seem to know how to get where we want to go. (Theories on community transformation have always been more abundant than successful case studies.) In an effort to remedy this confusion, our next chapter will offer some initial insights on the nature and benefits of spiritual mapping.

NOTES

1. God's practice of dealing distinctly with different cities is seen in the unique messages He spoke to the seven churches featured in Revelation chapters 2 and 3.

2. See Genesis 32:26; 1 Chronicles 16:11; Daniel 6:10; Luke 11:5-10; Hebrews 11:6; James 5:16.

3. In the early 1990s, a group of Japanese intercessors rented six railroad coaches, which they dubbed the "Glory Train," and rode the mobile prayer platform through all of Japan's prefectures.

4. Witchcraft is widespread in Pakistan. Initiates learn to control their emotions—particularly fear—during the course of intense encounters with demonic powers. During the final initiatory stage the demons appear in a variety of terrifying forms. If fear gets the best of the initiate, the demon(s) will kill him. If the initiate controls his fear, the demon(s) will be his to "command." The only requirement is that the initiate "entertain" the demon(s) every Thursday night. This entertainment takes the form of a ritual, known as *chowky*, which involves dancing and/or violent head and neck shaking (almost like seizures). Many witches die when they get older and are no longer able to fulfill their Thursday evening vows.

5. This time estimate is derived from Dr. C. Peter Wagner.

6. Robert Bakke, "Prayer: God's Catalyst for Revival," *Pray!*, Premier Issue, 1997, p. 16. Mr. Bakke directs the National Prayer Advance for the Evangelical Free Church in America.

7. Harold Caballeros, "Defeating the Enemy with the Help of Spiritual Mapping," in C. Peter Wagner's *Breaking Strongholds in Your City* (Ventura, CA: Regal, 1993), p. 144.

8. As I noted in my recent book *The Twilight Labyrinth* (Grand Rapids: Chosen, 1997), pp. 281, 282: In asking intercessors to petition God for an "open door," Paul is acknowledging three important truths: (1) Unsaved people are bound in a prison of deception; (2) God must breach this stronghold if the gospel is to enter; and (3) Prayer is an important means of persuading God to do this. If we want to practice effective spellbending—liberating enchanted minds so they can understand and respond to the gospel—we must first neutralize the blinding influence of demonic strongmen. Jesus talks about this process in Mark 3:27 when He says, "No one can enter a strong man's house (the human mind) and carry off his possessions unless he first ties up the strong man. *Then* he can rob his house" (emphasis added). We are not asking God to "make" people Christians, or to expel demonic powers that have become objects of worship. Such requests violate man's free will and God will not honor them. What we are appealing for is a level playing field, a temporary lifting of the spiritual blindness that prevents men from processing truth (the gospel) at a heart level.

9. Ibid., p. 300.
10. See Revelation 3:17.

Chapter 3

⁓

THE NATURE AND BENEFITS OF SPIRITUAL MAPPING

Reality can be a slippery customer. As soon as we think we have finally reeled it in from the deep, it wriggles off our line or changes into something altogether different. The impact on our psyche can be disconcerting.

In fact, it is not reality that has changed but rather our perspective. As the late Franco-American writer and diarist Anaïs Nin once observed: "We don't see things as they are. We see them as we are."

The questions are, What are we? What dominates our viewpoint? What colors our worldview? Is anything we see truly real?

If faulty vision is the first suspect to be questioned, it is not the only one. We must also investigate our speech, or social language. This is important because the language we use can directly influence our view of reality. In fact, there is a sense in which our language actually *creates* our reality. Studies have shown that whenever we spend an appreciable amount of time with certain people, we start to form a group language. This speech may be male or female, urban or rural, Black or Anglo, Western or Eastern, Presbyterian or Pentecostal, senior citizen or Generation X. Whatever the language, the longer it is spoken, the more it starts to define our reality. And once we begin to share a reality, we run the risk of becoming more and more closed off from new experiences.

Over time limited environments can occlude vision. Those who inhabit these environments begin to embrace the assumption that their limited field of view is all there is. Appearances become synonymous with reality.

I developed a fresh appreciation for this truth a few years ago when a glossy, four-fold advertisement arrived in my mailbox. The Sony Corporation, who it seemed was deeply concerned about my home entertainment needs, had reached out to me through one of their mass mailings. While my normal routine is to deposit such bulk-rate ads in the wastebasket, this particular sales piece caught my attention.

On the outside flap a single word—REALITY—was emblazoned amid a cluster of question marks. Intrigued, I lifted an intermediate flap to see where this teaser led. There in blue lettering spread across two panels were the words: IT'S ALL HOW YOU LOOK AT THINGS.

By now I was hooked (confirming, perhaps, the genius of the Sony marketing department). Opening a final inside flap I found myself staring at one of those popular, but confusing, three-dimensional images. Realizing the advertisement's punch line was hidden in a "noisy" pattern of small, seemingly insignificant objects, I rotated the page in search of a revealing angle.

Walking in on this amusing scene, my son Brendan exclaimed, "If you want to view that 3-D image, you'll have to cross your eyes."

I looked at him skeptically.

"I'm serious," he said. "Just place the page on the end of your nose and pull it back slowly."

As I followed this suspicious advice I couldn't help thinking about Naaman's dipfest in the Jordan River (see 2 Kings 5:9-14). Would my actions lead to revelation or humiliation?

It did not take long to find out. Lifting the image cautiously off my nose, I was enveloped immediately by a floating armada of Sony audio-video components. In some magnificent, mysterious way, I had "entered" the page!

After spending several moments marveling at the effect, I was struck by the fact that these images had been there all the time—I just hadn't *seen* them.

In this sense, my experience was similar to that of Elisha's servant at Dothan (see 2 Kings 6:8-18). When this young man noted with dismay that ruthless Aramean troops had surrounded his city, Elisha responded by asking God to "open his eyes so he may see" (verse 17). This was not out of a concern for the young man's natural vision. What he claimed to see was really there. The problem lay with what he did *not* see.

When the blinders were removed from his spiritual eyes, Elisha's servant discovered that the Aramean army was itself besieged by a fiery angelic host. Armed with this new perspective, he was able to reach a very different conclusion about his prospects.

Kofi Annan, the popular secretary general of the United Nations, also likes to talk about vision and perspective. In a recent interview with public talk-show host Charlie Rose, Annan revealed that while studying as a young man in West Africa, his headmaster showed him a large piece of paper with a small mark on it.

The headmaster asked, "What do you see?"

"I see a black dot," Annan replied.

Furrowing his brow, the headmaster exclaimed, "I'm holding up this huge piece of paper and all you see is a black dot! If you are going to get anywhere, Kofi, you must learn to open your eyes to the larger context of things."[1]

"Reality," as Salman Rushdie once explained on All-India Radio, "is a question of perspective; the further you get from the past, the more concrete and plausible it seems—but as you approach the present, it inevitably seems incredible."[2] This observation is especially relevant to the Church's view of the supernatural. A majority of Christians may be prepared to accept the biblical record of human interaction with the spiritual forces, but they are far less inclined to accept that reality today.

As I noted in *The Twilight Labyrinth*, Western Christianity has been clinging to its millpond discriminations of reality so tenaciously that it has nearly lost all ability to recognize the spiritual dimension. "We are," to quote William Irwin Thompson, "like flies crawling across the ceiling of the Sistine Chapel: we cannot see what angels and gods lie underneath the threshold of our perceptions. We do not live in reality; we live in our paradigms, our habituated perceptions, our illusions."[3]

According to some observers this posture is not only mistaken, it is indefensible. British Philosopher Karl Popper says simply, "I hold it to be morally wrong not to believe in reality."[4]

Why is this so? Because choosing to limit our perspective is an unnatural act. When God breathed "the breath of life" into Adam's nostrils (Gen. 2:7), He brought forth something utterly unique in creation—a being endowed with the capacity to traffic in two dimensions (the material and spiritual). Since "God is spirit" (John 4:24), He wanted to insure His children could relate to Him according to His nature. With this in mind the Almighty bent over Adam's dusty form and exhaled. The inside of God spawned life inside man. Humanity became a race of spirits.

Unfortunately, many people neglect to utilize their full range of endowments. Westerners, including a disconcerting number of Christians, are especially guilty of this. Having embraced the language and worldview of the Enlightenment, they dismiss spiritual vision as superstitious folly. Ask them to explain why things are the way they are in their communities, and they will instinctively turn to the oracles of sociology, economics or politics. Talk of spiritual explanations and you have bounded outside their comfort zone.

Like Elisha's servant, these individuals have become one-eyed jacks, able to discern material matters but blind to the spiritual realities standing behind them. They are like the man or woman who stands between two mirrors. Try as they might to peer into the cascading depths of infinity they find their vision blocked by their own head.

The problem here is a wrong assumption: namely, the material realm is the basement of reality. Unfortunately, wrong assumptions have a way of leading to wrong conclusions. If we are to succeed in our mission to further God's kingdom on earth, we must learn to see our communities as they *really* are, not merely as they *appear* to be. As Paul reminds us in Ephesians 6, our conflict is linked inextricably with dark supernatural powers. This being true, it does not make much sense for us to try and interpret our surroundings by natural means alone.

A NEW WAY OF SEEING

The discipline of spiritual mapping offers one of the best means of enhancing our perspective on reality. Its growing popularity among pastors, evangelists and intercessors bears strong witness to its effectiveness.

Unlike conventional interpretive devices, spiritual mapping does not confine itself to a single dimension. Rather, it works by superimposing our understanding of forces and events in the spiritual domain onto places and circumstances in the material world.[5]

Put simply, spiritual mapping enables us to "see" things that were previously undetectable with our natural eyes. In addition to angels and other divine resources (see 1 Kings 19:18; 2 Kings 6:17; Luke 24:31), these veiled realities can include repressed hurts (associated with unresolved social injustice), spiritual pacts (*quid pro quo* solutions to individual or corporate trauma) and demonic strongholds (both psychic and territorial) that daily hinder the advance of the gospel.

Good vision provides knowledge, and it is knowledge that allows us to distinguish one problem or condition from another. (The word "diagnosis" literally means "through knowledge" [Greek *dia* = "through" + *gnosis* = "knowledge"].) With its inherent diagnostic capacity, spiritual mapping empowers intercessors in much the same way that X-rays serve physicians.[6]

THE RATIONALE FOR SPIRITUAL MAPPING

Now that we have a better idea of what spiritual mapping is, it is time to consider whether this activity is really worth the time it requires.

This question—and it is a good one—is on the minds of many today. One Christian leader newly exposed to the discipline asked me a few years ago, "Why should I spend all this time doing research when I could be doing evangelism?" Her tone was not hostile, just honest.

"Let me respond," I said softly, "by asking you to tell me a little bit about your community. Are you currently experiencing a visitation of the Holy Spirit?"

"I wish we were," she replied.

I continued, "Are there any churches in the community?"

"Oh, there are dozens," she said matter-of-factly. "Most have modest attendance, but there are a few big ones."

I probed, "And how long have these churches been in the community?"

Pausing for a moment she replied, "Some have been here for more than a hundred years."

❧

THE *NEED* FOR SPIRITUAL MAPPING IS ROOTED IN ITS *PURPOSE*. LARGE-SCALE CONVERSIONS ARE UNLIKELY TO OCCUR UNLESS WE DISCERN THE NATURE AND ORIGIN OF OBSTACLES TO REVIVAL AND RECEIVE GOD'S PRESCRIBED STRATEGIES FOR THEIR REMOVAL.

❧

After continuing this line of inquiry for another minute or two, I said, "Let me see if I can summarize what you have told me. Although there are dozens of churches in your community—including some that have been around for more than a century—

you are not experiencing anything that could be called a revival or evangelistic breakthrough. Is that about the size of things?"

When my friend sadly shook her head in agreement, I said, "That's why you need to do spiritual mapping."

Reasonable research is research for a reason. We engage in spiritual mapping because we, like this dear Christian lady, wish to see our communities transformed by the power of the Holy Spirit. In this sense, the *need* for spiritual mapping is rooted in its *purpose*. Large-scale conversions are unlikely to occur unless we discern the nature and origin of any obstacles to revival and receive God's prescribed strategies for their removal.

Spiritual mapping can be a boon to anyone who has experienced the frustration of developing evangelistic strategies that never seem to work. Though it is not a substitute for passionate prayer or evangelism, it can make both considerably more effective.

DETAILED INFORMATION SUSTAINS FERVENT PRAYER

Revelation is the paintbrush God uses to enliven the gray canvas of our everyday reality. Dabbed in the medium of information—details that sit on His palette like dollops of multi-hued paint—it yields to the Master's touch. With a few well-placed strokes, He liberates us from vagaries and boredom.

Seeing things as they truly are stirs us, even when the details themselves are dull or grim.[7] This is because God has designed our emotions to respond to what our mind is thinking about. When we are flooded with details, reality becomes intelligible. We call this emotionally satisfying event *understanding*.

Ambiguity and generalities have the opposite effect. Starved of detail, our mind and emotions shut down. There is no sense of momentum toward an ultimate solution. We have no place to go.

Ask a typical prayer group to join in fervent intercession for Nauru or Djibouti and they will gladly give you their time. For the first 20 minutes or so, the room will resonate with energy. The devil will be bound, the lost will be claimed, and God's blessings will be invoked. Somewhere around the 30-minute mark, however, the energy level will drop precipitously. The intercessors may want to maintain their intensity; they just don't know where Nauru is!

Breakthrough prayer requires information in the same manner that a steam locomotive must have its boiler stoked with coal. Details (or familiarity) engender fervency and perseverance; and it is earnest, *sustained prayer* that leads to results (see Luke 11:5-8; Jas. 5:16). Spiritual mapping is one of the best means of keeping the boiler stoked.

DETAILED INFORMATION LEADS TO ECONOMIC AND EFFECTIVE ACTION

Anyone needing to remove an old or unsafe structure would do well to call Controlled Demolition, Inc. Its owners, the Loizeaux family, have blown up more buildings than anyone alive—at least anyone with peaceful intentions. Their planned demolition work is so precise they can predict where, and how, a building will fall.

The art of causing a structure to collapse in on itself is called implosion, and according to Loizeaux experts the key to success is not how much explosive power is used, but where it is placed.[8]

So it is with effectual spiritual warfare. Although we have the power to overthrow kingdoms (see Jer. 1:10) and demolish strongholds (see 2 Cor. 10:4), this power must be discharged in a controlled manner. When the psalmist declares: "[God] trains my hands for war, my fingers for battle" (Psalm 144:1), the emphasis is on preparation and precision. Power alone is not enough to win the victory.

Any modern fighter pilot will tell you the same thing. Divorced from accurate targeting coordinates, supersonic aircraft and laser-guided missiles are merely expensive toys. It is the quality of intelligence, not raw horsepower, which ultimately determines a mission's impact.

MEANINGFUL INTELLIGENCE ON OUR COMMUNITIES
IS READILY OBTAINABLE THROUGH SPIRITUAL
MAPPING WHICH MAKES IT EASIER TO
ABANDON OUR PRIMITIVE HIT-AND-MISS
APPROACH TO SPIRITUAL WARFARE
(SOMETIMES CALLED THE PIÑATA METHOD).

Fortunately, God has not left us to fight blind. Meaningful intelligence on our communities is readily obtainable through spiritual mapping. As we absorb the benefits of this Spirit-led research, it becomes easier to abandon our primitive hit-and-miss approach to spiritual warfare (sometimes called the piñata method). Fresh insight and understanding release us to economic and effective action.

DELIVERING PRACTICAL INSIGHTS

Before any minister of the gospel attempts to determine what he or she must do to achieve breakthroughs in a given community, he or she must first try to understand why things are the way they are. Here are two examples of how spiritual mapping helped local believers gain the practical insights they needed.

UNRAVELING THE MYSTERY OF RIO RANCHO
In early 1988 a young denominational pastor sensed a call to plant a church in Rio Rancho, a growing community north of Albuquerque, New Mexico. When he shared his thoughts with his supervisor, however, the reaction was not what he had expected. Instead of offering a congratulatory slap on the back, his mentor challenged him with the failed accounts of several predecessors.

This got the young man to thinking. He suspected there might be more to this story than met the eye. Given Rio Rancho's close proximity to the Indian pueblos of Zia and Santa Ana, he wondered if there might be some carry-over baggage from the past.

In the course of his research, he stumbled across a detailed account of a Zia man who had been converted and filled with the Holy Ghost in March of 1939.[9] The man had witnessed openly for several months before being summoned by tribal elders. During his "hearing" he was chastised for departing from the ways of his fathers and adopting a foreign religion. When he refused to recant his faith, the elders canceled his membership in the pueblo, deprived him of land and water, and forbade him to speak any further about Christianity.

The pueblo leaders also took action to prohibit evangelical churches from being planted in the vicinity of the reservation. While some of these measures were administrative in nature, there is also evidence that a spiritual curse may have been placed on adjacent lands—including Rio Rancho. This was reportedly done to create a buffer against evangelical Christianity and in retaliation for the white man's encroachment upon traditional Zia hunting and burial grounds.[10]

Armed with this intelligence, local intercessors went to prayer. A breakthrough was recorded in 1993 when a medicine man attached to the Santa Ana pueblo was born again. This led to the subsequent conversion of about 30 others, including several tribal leaders and families from adjacent pueblos.[11] At the same time, a number of large evangelical churches began to spring up in Rio Rancho.

THE OLD BONES OF HSINCHU

In his book, *The Collapse of the Brass Heaven,* Zeb Bradford Long describes an experience he and his wife Laura had while serving as missionary trainers in Taiwan.

Their assignment had brought them to the Presbyterian Bible College at Hsinchu, a city on the island's northwest coast.

According to Long:

> The school had one foot in the grave; the buildings and grounds bore a look of decay. The student body was down to sixty and losing more. The faculty was laced with contention. The prevailing opinion was that the place should be closed and the buildings sold.
>
> Coldness and hostility filled the atmosphere. Even on a beautiful day with a clear blue sky and blooming azaleas, one had to fight depression. Many people complained of this. One Taiwanese pastor told us that the one hour he taught there was the most difficult hour of the week. He always left with a feeling of deep oppression.[12]

In September 1982 Long attended a prayer retreat in Chiai, in southern Taiwan. As the participants directed their attention to the problems affecting the Bible college, a man from New Zealand, with apparently no knowledge of the school, cried out suddenly, "Old bones, old bones!" This was followed by several visions concerning the supernatural conflict that was raging around the institution.

Subsequent to the Chiai meeting, research revealed that the land on which the college was built was once a Buddhist crematorium and cemetery. The original Chinese landowners, believing the property to be haunted by spirits, were quite happy to sell it off to the foreign missionaries. This confirmed to Long and his associates that the reference to old bones was not simply metaphorical.

As various intercessors conducted educated prayer walks around the campus, the oppression that had been plaguing the school began to dissipate. In time, says Long, "the Holy Spirit came with new power," paving the way for [a] lay training center, which eventually brought healing and deliverance to many.[13]

DOCTRINES AND PRECEDENTS

In spite of examples like these, some Christians have expressed concern over what they consider to be a biblically uncredentialed discipline. Some have gone so far as to call spiritual mapping (and spiritual warfare) the "new magic" or "Christian animism."

More often than not, however, these conclusions are based on limited encounters with the practice. As critics take a second look, most are relieved to learn that the discipline is actually a close relative of both cultural geography and cultural anthropology.

Those who retain their skepticism cite spiritual mapping's unabashed acknowledgment of active supernatural forces (both demonic and divine), and its recognition of prayer as a legitimate methodology for data collection. In their ordered world, there is simply no room to indulge in such loose and unscientific thinking.

But is this the last word? Are we really meant to play by Enlightenment rules? Is New Testament-style supernaturalism passé? Has God muted His voice to contemporary generations?

THE SUPERNATURAL ASPECT OF SPIRITUAL WARFARE

In responding to these questions, our initial task is to solicit a scriptural perspective on spiritual warfare. What exactly are we dealing with in our communities? Is the problem limited to bad choices and bad thinking, or is there something else at work?

In Luke 10:19 Jesus told His disciples, "I have given you authority to trample on snakes and scorpions and to *overcome all the power of the enemy*" (emphasis added). While some have endeavored to define this powerful enemy as arguments or philosophies, the reference to demons in verse 17 is unambiguous. Christ is instructing His followers to employ supernatural power to overcome supernatural beings.

This teaching is reinforced in Matthew 12:22-29. Speaking of Beelzebub, the prince of demons, Jesus asked, "How can anyone enter a strong man's house and carry off his possessions unless he first ties up the strong man?" (verse 29). The implication here is that if we want to liberate spiritual captives we must first subdue the occupying demonic power.[14]

The apostle Paul accentuates this supernatural aspect of our warfare in Ephesians 6:12 when he reminds us that "our struggle is not against flesh and blood, but against...spiritual forces of evil in the heavenly realms."

Other references to the reality of cosmic forces and/or the importance of spiritual warfare can be found in 1 Chronicles 21:1; Job 1; Daniel 10; Acts 13:4-12; Ephesians 6:10-20; 1 Peter 5:8; and Revelation 12:12.

THE LEGITIMACY OF DIVINE REVELATION

If spiritual forces are an active part of our campaign to liberate lost men and women, it should not surprise us that God—the most potent force of all—would occasionally reveal useful secrets and strategies.

In God's economy, revelation flows out of relationship. Christ calls us by name and leads us out. We follow Him because we "know his voice" (John 10:4). This process is both intimate and natural. "Whether you turn to the right or to the left," Isaiah explains, "your ears will hear a voice behind you, saying, 'This is the way; walk in it'" (Isa. 30:21).

The power and practicality of this experience should not be underestimated. When Paul and his companions "came to the border of Mysia, they tried to enter Bithynia, but the Spirit of Jesus would not allow them to" (Acts 16:7). A few nights later the apostle "had a vision of a man of Macedonia standing and begging him, 'Come over to Macedonia and help us'" (verse 9). As a result of this strategic redirection, many new churches were planted in the region of modern-day Greece.

While divine revelation is often dramatic, it is not uncommon. In fact, Amos informs us that "the Sovereign Lord does nothing without revealing his plan to his servants the prophets" (Amos 3:7). When Joshua urged Moses to forbid Eldad and Medad from prophesying in the camp of the Israelites, his mentor replied, "Are you jealous for my sake? I wish that all the Lord's people were prophets and that the Lord would put his Spirit on them!" (Num. 11:29).

In his first epistle to the church at Corinth, Paul admonishes his readers to "Follow the way of love and eagerly desire spiritual gifts, especially the gift of prophecy" (1 Cor. 14:1). "When you come together," he adds, "*everyone* [should have] a hymn, or a word of instruction, a *revelation,* a tongue or an interpretation" (verse 26, emphasis added).[15]

Given the content and tone of these passages, there would appear to be no intrinsic reason for us to reject divine revelation as a legitimate source of information. God's communication with His friends should not be seen as magic, but as normal behavior. As our daily guide and confidant, He is as interested in the details of modern life as He is in the doctrines of the New Covenant (see Job 1:10; Psalms 1:6; 37:23; Luke 12:6,7,22-31).[16]

This is not to suggest that our interpretations of God's disclosures are impervious to human error. Mistakes are inevitable. To insure they do not lead us astray we should test our conclusions against Scripture, mature counsel, and objective evidence gleaned through historical review, sociological observation and statistical analysis.

BIBLICAL PRECEDENTS FOR SPIRITUAL MAPPING
We must also consider the charge that spiritual mapping is a contemporary invention devoid of biblical precedent. If this were found to be true, it would certainly give us reason for pause.

Fortunately, God's Word offers up several precedents for spiritual mapping. While some purists may find these to be underdeveloped, anyone familiar with God's history of adapting to the age will discern unmistakable roots.

The first example is found in Numbers 13 where Moses, at God's behest, dispatched spies into Canaan to "see what the land is like" (verse 18). The expedition lasted 40 days and included a detailed research agenda. (At least eight discovery questions were assigned to the scouts.) The fact that God was already well acquainted with Canaan's challenges testifies to the importance He places on human interaction with spiritual strongholds. In this case, there were implications for an entire nation.

A similar account of territorial surveying is recorded in Joshua 18. Here the great veteran of the original Canaan expedition sent out 21 agents from Shiloh "to make a survey of the land and to write a description of it" (verse 4). As the men left "to map out the land" Joshua instructed them to "[write] its description on a scroll, town by town, in seven parts" (verses 8,9). On the basis of this thorough research, the land of inheritance was divided up among seven Israelite tribes.

Spiritual reconnaissance was also undertaken in Jericho when Joshua commissioned two spies to go "look over the land" (Josh. 2:1), and in Jerusalem when Nehemiah conducted three days of research prior to restoring the city's walls.

> And I arose in the night, I and some few men with me; neither told I any man what my God had put in my heart to do at Jerusalem....And I went out by night by the gate of the valley, even before the dragon well, and to the dung port, and viewed the walls of Jerusalem, which were broken down, and the gates thereof were consumed with fire. Then I went on to the gate of the fountain, and to the king's pool....Then went I up in the night by the brook, and viewed the wall, and turned back, and entered by the gate of the valley, and so returned (Neh. 2:12-15, *KJV*).

In Acts 17 we run into spiritual mapping again, this time in connection with Paul's sojourn in Athens. While waiting for Timothy and Silas to join him, the apostle was "greatly distressed to see that the city was full of idols" (verse 16).

With a heavy heart and time on his hands, the great missionary seized the occasion to investigate local sites and customs.

Besides interacting with Epicurean and Stoic philosophers (see verses 17-21), he also managed to digest the works of Greek poets (see verse 28). Later, in his famous Mars Hill address, Paul declared, "Men of Athens! I see that in every way you are very religious. For as I walked around and looked carefully at your objects of worship, I even found an altar with this inscription: TO AN UNKNOWN GOD" (verses 22,23).

While there is no explicit evidence that the apostle took the results of this urban reconnaissance into spiritual warfare—specifically prayer against prevailing spiritual powers—we may speculate that he did. To start with, we know that Paul was a man of prayer (see Acts 21:5; Rom. 1:9,10) and that he was "greatly distressed" by the Athenians' devotion to idols. We also know that he understood the relationship between idols and demonic powers (see 1 Cor. 10:19-21) and that he recognized these powers as the focal point of our spiritual struggle (see Eph. 6:12). As he made plans to penetrate the deceptive strongholds erected by these demons, Paul implored the church at Colosse to pray for an open door (see Col. 4:2,3).

Even if the apostle did not engage the powers at Athens, he clearly used spiritual mapping intelligence in fashioning his evangelistic appeal to the Areopagus. As a result of this decision, Paul's preaching led to several notable conversions—including that of Dionysius, a member of the Athenian supreme court.

A more oblique reference to spiritual mapping is found in Ezekiel 8. In this memorable chapter, the prophet describes an intense and disturbing vision. Yielding to the Spirit's direction, he is taken to Jerusalem's Temple court where he is instructed to dig through a hole in the wall. Upon entering a secret doorway on the other side, he is shocked to find the elders of Israel engaged in idolatrous and perverse worship (see verses 7-11).

After drawing Ezekiel's attention to this hidden abomination, God leads the prophet past the north gate of the temple where women are weeping for the Babylonian fertility god,

Tammuz. "Do you see this, son of man?" He asks. "You will see things that are even more detestable than this" (verse 15).

The site of this ultimate desecration proved to be the inner court of the temple. There, between the portico and the altar, the prophet observed 25 men bowing down to worship the eastern sun (see verse 16).

As Ezekiel carried this new understanding into passionate intercession, he was given a series of divine instructions designed to deliver Israel from her bondage to the doctrines of demons. These liberating measures included revelatory prophecies (see 11:5), symbolic acts (see 12:3-6), and the preaching of repentance (see 14:6).[17]

A TIMELY EMPHASIS

In spite of evidence that spiritual mapping is both biblical and useful, some critics insist the practice is nothing more than the latest fad.[18] Given time, they contend, reasonable people will abandon it in favor of more proven ministry methodologies.

The difficulty with this position is that it neglects to distinguish between a passing fancy and a divine emphasis. Whereas human fads can be trivial, divine emphases are timely responses to prevailing needs or circumstances. The fact that they are short-lived or a reprise of an earlier theme says nothing about their origin or value.

It is myopic to dismiss spiritual mapping simply because it has not always been at the forefront of church growth strategy. Christian broadcasting was unknown prior to the twentieth century, yet few would deny its legitimacy or effectiveness. The same could be said of the modern emphasis on unreached people groups and the 10/40 Window. Until recently, these concepts were not even in our mission vocabulary.[19]

While we may find such discontinuity intimidating, God does not. Change is part of His design. As a dynamic and creative Sovereign, He is well able to adapt to the peculiarities of each age and culture.[20] Every fresh move of His Spirit presents us with new emphases, new methods, new leaders and new vocabulary.

This process is clearly observable in the introduction of the Mosaic Covenant (see Exod. 19—24), the baptism of John (see Matt. 3:5,6; Acts 13:24), Jesus' emphasis on the kingdom of God (see Luke 17:21; John 3:5,6), and Peter's revelation about God's willingness to pour out His Spirit upon the Gentiles (see Acts 10). It is also seen in the teachings of Paul, the theological wind shifts of the Reformation, and the radical lifestyle of the Moravians.

SPIRITUAL MAPPING—WHY NOW?

More recently, the impulse of God's Spirit has given rise to movements championing everything from spiritual gifts and holiness to faith and church growth. Each of these emphases, despite the imperfections of certain messengers, has left a timely and helpful deposit in the life of the Church. Today the heavenly trade winds are bearing a fresh emphasis on intercessory prayer and spiritual warfare. Like others before it, this latest stirring is accompanied by a number of foreign-sounding terms—most notably *strategic-level spiritual warfare, identificational repentance* and *spiritual mapping* (one could also add prophetic intercession and solemn assemblies). Although none of these concepts is without precedent (see Josh. 18:8,9; Dan. 9:20; Eph. 6:12), each is experiencing a dramatic renaissance.

The salient question is, *Why now?*

To honest seekers, the answer seems obvious. We have entered the most complex and turbulent period in human history. An explosion of knowledge (see Dan. 12:4) has ushered in a brave new world of electronic stimulation and human cloning. Breakthroughs in global evangelization (see Matt. 24:14) have triggered unprecedented demonic activity (see Rev. 12:12). Spiritual mapping makes good sense now because the end times have become our times.

THE DOUBLE-SIDED TOOLBOX

As a just and loving sovereign, God never leaves His people without hope. He always provides the resources that are necessary to meet the challenges at hand. On some occasions, this involves revealing critical information, while other situations call for special power or protection.

Our day is no different. To help us deal with the unique and daunting realities of twenty-first century ministry, God has prepared a dual-compartment tool kit. On one side, labeled "Tools of the Ages," we find disciplines like faith, humility and holiness that are essential to success in all times and places. In the opposite compartment, we find the "Tools of the Hour." These are special keys (like spiritual mapping) that can unlock the defining bondages of the day (including information overload and intense demonic counterfeits).

The importance of these *tools of the hour* was first impressed upon me in the early 1990s. The occasion was a spiritual warfare seminar I had been invited to conduct for a group of Presbyterian missionaries at Bryan College in Tennessee. At the conclusion of one of my sessions, a gentleman who introduced himself as Philip Foxwell approached me. He proved to be a man with quite a story.

Prior to entering missionary service in Japan, Foxwell had won the grand prize trophy at the International Brotherhood of Magicians Convention in 1937. To display his talents—commercial television was still in its infancy—he maintained a rigorous tour schedule that involved thousands of stage performances in every corner of the United States.

Foxwell's specialty was escapes, a trick that can be risky even when careful preparations are made. As an example of these perils, Foxwell cited a performance in Midland, Michigan, in which he was to extricate himself from a pair of police-issue handcuffs.

"In those days," Foxwell told me, "most police departments used Peerless brand cuffs, including the Midland sheriff's office.

Since I had studied these in the lock shop, I anticipated no difficulty with my upcoming escape.

"But a shock was in store. When the sheriff bounded dramatically onto the stage, he produced a new model of Peerless cuffs I had never seen before. Had I not managed to surreptitiously acquire the sheriff's key, I might still be locked in those cuffs! *Knowledge has to be combined with the appropriate hardware.*"[20]

In similar fashion, spiritual mapping can be an exceedingly valuable tool in the hands of Christians desiring to unlock obstacles to revival in their communities. The main difference is that this versatile key can open with equal virtuosity shackles forged of ancient superstition or the latest deceptive alloys.

Like any tool, however, this "appropriate hardware" saves its best results for those who have learned to use it correctly. Quality preparation leads to realized potential—and for those who are interested, the instruction manual is no more than a page turn away.

NOTES

1. "Charlie Rose," PBS, May 2, 1997.
2. Salman Rushdie, *Midnight's Children* (New York: A. A. Knopf, 1981), n.p., as heard on "All-India Radio."
3. George Otis, Jr., *The Twilight Labyrinth* (Grand Rapids: Chosen, 1997), p. 64.
4. Quoted by Lance Morrow in "The Trouble with the Present Tense," *Time*, (March 30, 1998), n.p.
5. George Otis, Jr., *The Last of the Giants* (Grand Rapids: Chosen, 1991), p. 85.
6. Harold Caballeros, senior pastor of El Shaddai Church in Guatemala City, was the first to present this analogy.
7. As I mentioned in chapter 2, revelation is a potent stimulus of fervent intercession. Only answered prayer can generate a comparable level of intensity and enthusiasm.
8. "The Discovery Channel, Discovery Sunday," *Blast Force*, May 11, 1997.
9. Leslie White, *The Pueblo of Zia, New Mexico* (Washington, D.C.: U.S. Government Print Office, 1962), reprinted 1995, n.p.
10. Developers in Rio Rancho often unearth Indian ruins and artifacts. Many contractors will cover these up quickly to avoid costly construction delays. Indeed one individual I spoke to reported seeing an ancient *kiva* (underground ritual chamber made of stone or mud) complete with ashes from a ceremonial fire. A few weeks later the site was level ground.

11. Confidential correspondence from an area pastor and a Native American source dated December 1, 1994.

12. Zeb Bradford Long and Douglas McMurry, *The Collapse of the Brass Heaven* (Grand Rapids: Chosen, 1994), p. 194.

13. Ibid., p. 195.

14. For more on this topic see Otis, *The Twilight Labyrinth*, pp. 280-283.

15. See also Daniel 9:20-22; Acts 11:27,28; 19:1-7.

16. See also Psalm 48:14; 73:24; Ecclesiastes 2:26a; Isaiah 42:16.

17. Second Kings 20 presents a nasty example of enemy reconnaissance. In this account Israel's king Hezekiah received emissaries from the Babylonian monarch, Merodach-Baladan. While the messengers were in Jerusalem Hezekiah carelessly gave them a complete tour of his treasury, palace and armory. Catching wind of this, the prophet Isaiah asked the king: "What did they [the messengers] see in your palace?" (verse 15). When Hezekiah replied that he had hidden nothing from the Babylonian emissaries, Isaiah declared, "Hear the word of the Lord: The time will surely come when everything in your palace, and all that your fathers have stored up until this day, will be carried off to Babylon. Nothing will be left" (verses 16,17).

18. Art Moore, "Spiritual Mapping Gains Credibility Among Leaders," *Christianity Today*, (January 12, 1998), n.p.; Robert Zend displayed a similar attitude in the August 1994 issue of *The Reader's Digest*: "Being a philosopher," he wrote, "I have a problem for every solution."

19. In my 1991 book, *The Last of the Giants*, I wrote: History is not prescriptive; and as one astute writer has pointed out, "Neither heroism nor invention emerged from doing things as one did them in the past." For progress to be achieved in the spiritual or any other arena of life, prevailing assumptions about what is necessary and possible must be periodically challenged—not out of a juvenile desire to be deliberately provocative, but rather from the understanding that times change and that many assumptions held widely in the past have proven faulty and inaccurate (p. 260).

20. History, it should be remembered, is a river, not a pond. Each era represents a unique stretch along the highway of life. For this reason, the pace and scenery observed by our spiritual forefathers cannot be compared to present-day experiences. We are navigating a different place.

21. Philip Foxwell, *Missionary Magician* (Pasadena, CA: William Carey Library, 1989), pp. 28, 29.

RESEARCH LEVELS AND BOUNDARIES

For some years now there has been a measure of public uncertainty about what actually constitutes spiritual mapping. Many apply the term to any research that facilitates prayer for specific peoples, places or social networks. Others insist it is a corollary discipline of prayerwalking. Still others reserve the definition for systematic projects targeted at community transformation.

In reality, things need not be so confusing. The description of spiritual mapping given in chapter 3 fits any and all of these activities. Apparent differences lie not with the activity itself but with its products.

Spiritual mapping is, by its very nature, a multilayered discipline. Its products can include neighborhood or people-group profiles, various specialized briefings, and full-blown reports on given cities or regions. It can yield fascinating and helpful "character maps" that allow intercessors to view a community or territory the way God sees it.

Levels of Spiritual Mapping										
	Territorial Targets				Cultural Targets		Targets Social Targets			
	Neighborhoods	Cities & Towns	States & Provinces	Nations & Continents	People Groups	Religious Groups	Business & Industry	School Campuses	Military Facilities	Gov't. Institutions
Prayerwalking Profiles	✓	✓			✓	✓	✓	✓	✓	✓
Special Briefings	✓	✓			✓	✓	✓	✓	✓	✓
Community Reports	✓	✓			✓		✓	✓	✓	✓
Regional Reports			✓	✓	✓					
Character Maps	✓	✓	✓	✓			✓	✓	✓	✓

Figure 4.1

As the preceding chart (see Figure 4.1) illustrates, it is possible to construct a reference matrix highlighting potential spiritual mapping products. The vertical scale lists the primary *types of research output* (profiles, briefings, reports and maps), while the horizontal axis distinguishes various *research themes*. The latter includes territorial emphases (neighborhoods, cities, states, and nations), cultural targets (people groups and religions), and various social networks (industries, schools, and government institutions).

While thematic options are numerous, there are only four basic types of spiritual mapping products. In the next few pages we'll take a closer look at each of them.

PROFILES AND BRIEFINGS: BUILDING COMMUNITY AWARENESS

The first two types of spiritual mapping products—profiles and briefings—are designed primarily to build awareness of a given prayer need or opportunity. The particular target can be a local neighborhood, an unreached people group or a college campus. Users include anyone with a potential concern or burden for the featured target.

The simple structure and brief contents of these documents speak to their introductory nature. By design many important questions are not even raised, let alone answered. The objective is to stimulate an appetite for intercession, not sustain a lengthy prayerfest.

PRAYERWALKING PROFILES
One of the most common uses of spiritual mapping profiles is as an aid to prayerwalking. Literally millions of believers have taken intercessory walks or journeys in recent years. Some have linked up with international campaigns like the Reconciliation Walk, Praying Through the Window or the March for Jesus. Many oth-

ers have confined themselves to their own neighborhoods. Nearly all have used or sought some type of informational resource to help maximize their experience.

The best profiles are usually produced by local churches and ministries based in or near the target area. Although these products are brief, typically no longer than a couple of pages, they are infused with the love and concern that comes of vested interest and personal commitment.

Prayerwalking profiles can be developed in as little as two to four weeks—if the research team is diligent in its business. While a format for these guides has not been standardized, most include at least some treatment of local history, social bondages and spiritual competition. They also present a brief overview of current problems facing the body of Christ (e.g., apathy, persecution or disunity).

A final element incorporated into many profiles (often as a separate insert) is an actual prayerwalking itinerary. The most useful of these include:

1. A simple but accurate map including a dotted tour pathway and numbered prayer sites;
2. A description of relevant sites (i.e., pilgrimage shrines, Masonic temples, New Age bookstores);
3. Small photographs to help prayerwalkers recognize specific sites;
4. Practical miscellany (i.e., site entrance fees, known risk factors, local ordinance considerations, seasonal weather conditions);
5. Instructions about how to pray at the various sites.

SPECIAL BRIEFINGS
The second type of spiritual mapping product is the special briefing. Unlike profiles that are intended primarily for individual use,

this research package is designed for corporate consumption. Its purpose is to alert local churches, ministry teams and prayer groups to issues and circumstances that warrant special attention.

Although special briefings will occasionally be circulated through an entire network or community, they are more likely to be developed by, and for, a particular institution. Local church prayer ministries will often prepare such briefings for the benefit of (and often at the behest of) senior leadership. The intent, once again, is to apprise a particular congregation or ministry constituency of serious concerns or special opportunities.

Like prayer profiles, briefings can be developed relatively quickly and need not be put into a standardized format. Subject matter can deal with disturbing trends (such as the renewal of ancient spiritual practices), chronic problems (such as a lack of church growth in a given neighborhood) or unique circumstances (such as new openness to the gospel brought on by traumatic events).

FULL-SCALE REPORTS: STIMULATING COLLECTIVE ACTION

Spiritual mapping reports are distinguishable from their research siblings in both structure (they are bigger and highly standardized) and purpose (they are intended to stimulate collective action toward community transformation). These notable differences place them at the top of the spiritual mapping product line.

Given the high degree of commitment required at this level of spiritual mapping (projects can easily take two years to complete), there are comparatively few full-scale reports in circulation. Although some researchers have tried to substitute lesser efforts—most frequently mislabeled profiles or briefings—I know of no instance where these have led to the transformation of communities.

The role of spiritual mapping reports is not to stimulate an appetite for community intercession but rather to satisfy a hunger that already exists. There is nothing introductory about these research products. They are comprehensive analyses of complex social entities. Unlike profiles and briefings, they are meant to sustain lengthy prayer campaigns.

NEIGHBORHOOD REPORTS

The most common reports feature a specific town, neighborhood or gathering place. These can be produced by a local congregation, or by a coalition of ministries. Their purpose, as I noted above, is to sustain fervent corporate intercession until community transformation becomes a reality. The process of constructing these neighborhood reports is the primary focus of this book.

The definition of "neighborhood (or community) reports" is flexible enough to encompass any localized setting where people live, gather or display a common affinity. Examples include small towns, school campuses, Native reservations, large companies, housing estates, military bases or a particular city block. When the target area becomes too large in terms of either territory or population density, it no longer qualifies as a neighborhood report. The critical key is localization in making this determination.

In addition, neighborhood reports, unlike profiles and briefings, must be assembled according to a standardized design. There can be no deviation. Among the many reasons for this is the fact that spiritual mapping reports are part of a cause and effect process. If you want to see your community transformed by the power of the Holy Spirit, then you must find a way to sustain fervent corporate intercession. As I noted in chapter 2, one of the best means of achieving this is through progressive revelation. Spiritual mapping reports can help, but only if they follow certain rules. Appropriate questions must be asked—and then answered—in the proper sequence.

This same process is seen in industries ranging from engineering to agriculture. If a contractor wants to build a skyscraper, he must first acquire a set of reliable blueprints and then pour a solid foundation. If a farmer hopes to harvest a bumper crop, he must till the soil and plant and irrigate his seeds. Ignoring these tasks, or performing them out of sequence, will lead to hunger and disaster.

Another rationale for standardized reports is that they lend themselves to comparative analyses. This is particularly important in the detection of regional strongholds or spiritual patterns. By adopting a compatible system we are able to view issues and territories through the eyes of multiple observers, an approach that ensures a more complete and accurate assessment. Custom reports, on the other hand, are like a basket of mixed fruit; they may be impressive to the eye, but they cannot tell us much about the health of a particular crop.

Standard spiritual mapping reports include six sections, each dealing with a core topic like prevailing social bondages, the evolution of current circumstances, or the potential for spiritual breakthroughs (see chapter 6 for more details). The contents of these sections consist of answers to dozens of relevant discovery questions (see "Practical Resources" at end of this book for a complete list).

REGIONAL REPORTS

This type of mapping product enables Christians to discern the spiritual lay of the land in sprawling cities, counties, states or regions. It is the natural progression from the neighborhood or community report.

The scope of these "big picture" reports makes them both strategically valuable and difficult to produce. Too large for any single ministry to complete, they must be cobbled together over time by multi-church partnerships. The process requires patience and cooperation, virtues that are, unfortunately, in short supply.

Cali, Colombia, (population 2 million) presents a notable

and welcome exception to this pattern. When the city's church leaders decided to spiritually map their community in the mid-1990s, they divided this gargantuan assignment between dozens of local fellowships. In a scene reminiscent of the 41 Hebrew clans who rebuilt the walls of Jerusalem under Nehemiah,[1] each church took on the responsibility for investigating its immediate neighborhood. When these localized projects were completed several months later, the findings were then merged into one grand report.

Another cooperative research initiative, called the Northwest Corridor Project, was launched in the summer of 1998. This enormous campaign, still underway as of this writing, has mobilized hundreds of mappers between Alaska and Oregon for the purpose of investigating the spiritual dynamics at work in North America's most unchurched region. Working in cities, towns and reservations on both sides of the U.S.-Canadian border, mixed teams of Anglos and Native Americans are uncovering evidence of ancient migration routes, early spiritual pacts and a host of adaptive deceptions.

Other than size, regional reports are similar in structure to neighborhood reports. Both products deal with the same core questions and are intended to stimulate and sustain fervent corporate intercession.

CHARACTER MAPS: CREATING A VISIONARY STANDARD

Conventional city maps depict suburban neighborhoods or administrative districts as a patchwork of colors. A recent guide to the Los Angeles basin, for example, featured a brown Pasadena, a pink Hollywood, a yellow Long Beach and an orange Anaheim. A road map of Sydney, Australia, used the same colors to highlight the communities of Strathfield, Bondi, Epping and Parramatta.

As handy as these schemes may be for tourists, they offer little of substance to the intercessor. There is no way of knowing, for instance, whether the people who live in the pink district are any different from those who pursue their business in the yellow sector. We are left clueless as to what the boundary line between them really means.

In truth, many geopolitical boundaries, especially in the Western world, have no social or spiritual significance whatsoever. They are the arbitrary demarcations of faceless bureaucrats, the tired legacy of self-serving politicians. They divide without describing.

While at first glance this may appear to be no big deal, the matter becomes graver when we consider that these flimsy and arbitrary distinctions form the basis for many of our prayer initiatives. We may be talking to God about things that He does not recognize or that have no bearing in the spiritual dimension.

Like profiles, briefings and reports, character maps are designed to help intercessors see their communities as they really are (the divine viewpoint), not merely as they appear to be. They accomplish this mission by offering a practical alternative to conventional maps and geopolitical boundaries.

The first step in creating a character map is to ask what God sees when He looks at a given community. How does He distinguish one neighborhood or area from another? If conventional geopolitical boundaries are not always the best way to define reality, what is?

According to Scripture, God's primary focus is on the human heart (see 1 Sam. 16:7). He scrutinizes its fruit (see 2 Sam. 22:21-25; Jer. 17:10; Matt. 7:17-20; Luke 6:43-45) and searches out the object of its affection (see 1 Kings 11:1-4; 2 Chron. 16:9; Jer. 20:12; Ezek. 6:9, 14:3; Luke 12:34). Superficial actions and appearances mean very little (see Matt. 7:21-23; 23:25-29; Jas. 2:2-4).

Cities, nations and people groups are measured in the same way, only on a grander scale. At this level, God's attention is fixed on collective intent, collective allegiance and collective patterns of behavior. Individuals may deviate from the collective—witness Noah, Moses and Daniel—but they cannot obscure its essential traits and character.[2] In the end, the community will be known, and judged, by its fruit (see Gen. 18:20,21; Amos 9:8; Zeph. 1:12; Rev. 2—3).

From God's perspective, then, it is the character of a place that distinguishes it. Community boundaries are fixed not by bureaucrats and politicians but by moral choices and resulting patterns of behavior. What counts is what people worship.

Demonic powers also recognize these truths. When the devil offered Jesus "the kingdoms of the world" (Luke 4:5) it was a not-so-subtle boast that countless human communities were already flying his colors. The Scriptures acknowledge as much in passages like 2 Kings 17:29 and Jeremiah 2:28. He gained control of these communities then, as he does now, through *quid pro quo* pacts with local inhabitants.[3] In return for his promise to provide riches, power and protection, he garnered their full and ongoing allegiance.

As I explained in *The Twilight Labyrinth*:

Early Mesopotamian city-states like Babylon, Ur, and Nippur were considered the property of particular deities who ruled them as they saw fit. The same was true in Egypt, where every town, village and district had its god that bore the title *Lord of the City*. In Syria and Palestine, these local gods were called Baals, an appellation that signified their mastery over specific territories and communities.[4]

Cities like Ashtaroth, No Amon, Baal Gad and Athens adopted the actual names of their spiritual patrons. Others, like Ephesus, simply basked in their reputation.

The city clerk quieted the crowd and said: "Men of Ephesus, doesn't all the world know that the city of

Ephesus is the guardian of the temple of the great Artemis and of her image, which fell from heaven?" (Acts 19:35).

In linking Ephesus's identity to its spiritual allegiance and social reputation, this early civil servant offers up an outstanding example of character mapping. He is telling his audience, in so many words, that Ephesus is really "Artemis City." It is the goddess, not the government, which puts the city on the map.

Of course, God's perspective on such matters is often deeper, and more explicit, than that conveyed by public opinion. Babylon, whose name means, "Gate of the gods," is a case in point. Although maps and headlines of the day doubtless portrayed the city as a leading center of politics, education and religion, God saw it as "a home for demons and a haunt for every evil spirit" (Rev. 18:2). His character description for Babylon was the "Mother of Harlots" (Rev. 17:5, *KJV*). Nineveh was reidentified as "the mistress of sorceries" (Nah. 3:4), while Pergamum became known as the seat of Satan (see Rev. 2:13, *KJV*).

If we want to do spiritual work, it behooves us to start with a spiritual perspective. And since conventional maps are inadequate to this task, we need something new. We need character maps.

Two key elements distinguish these specialized maps: *descriptive names* and *meaningful boundaries*. To come up with the former, researchers will need to investigate the community's spiritual commitments, social reputation and any ongoing patterns of behavior. Meaningful clues are generally easy to spot. Take Athens, for example. The Bible tells us that while Paul waited for Silas and Timothy to join him in the Greek capital, "he was greatly distressed to see that the city was full of idols" (Acts 17:16). Further insight into the prevailing culture is provided in verse 21 where we learn:

All the Athenians and the foreigners who lived there

spent their time doing nothing but talking about and listening to the latest ideas.

This process of identification, or reidentification, is not always negative. After Jacob awoke from a heavenly vision near the city of Luz, he renamed the place Bethel, meaning "house of God" (Gen. 28:19; 35:15). When he encountered an angel at the Jabbok River, he called the site Peniel, or the "face of God" (Gen. 32:30). The prophet Zechariah proclaimed that on the Lord's return to Zion, "Jerusalem will be called the City of Truth" (Zech. 8:3).

Character mapping also requires us to redraw meaningful boundaries, be they around cities, nations or neighborhoods. An important starting point for this survey work is an examination of the spiritual worldview and allegiance of local inhabitants. Why is this so important? Because as William Robertson Smith observed in *The Religion of the Semites*, "The land of a god corresponds with the land of his worshipers."[5] Spiritual powers pitch their tents wherever they are welcomed by the tribal will.

Social reputation and chronic behavioral patterns should also be considered. Is a particular community known for its sexual indulgence such as Amsterdam's Red Light District, Bangkok's Pat Pong, Rio's Copacabana or New Orleans' French Quarter? Does a city's reputation and behavioral patterns such as Mixco, Guatemala,[6] or the town of Sedona, Arizona, attract cults? Is it a neighborhood or district that is prone to excessive crime (West Miami, East Los Angeles), poverty (Calcutta, Haiti) or suicide (Inuit Reservations in Canada and Alaska)?

In many metropolitan areas, these types of neighborhoods are mixed in with financial centers, university districts and religious suburbs. Unfortunately, they are rarely labeled for what they are. Instead, mapmakers follow the lead of politicians and bureaucrats, affixing names and boundaries that mean little to readers and even less to the spirit world. The only remedy for these artificial designations is a prayerfully prepared character map.

In recent years these and other spiritual mapping products have emerged as powerful reality-viewing instruments. They have become the orbiting Hubble telescope of community intercession. They have increased the vision of intercessors by lifting them above the distorting effects of the surrounding atmosphere.

WHAT SPIRITUAL MAPPING *ISN'T*

If spiritual mapping allows us to see beneath (or beyond) the surface of the material world, it is not magic. It does not create or manipulate reality. It is subjective only in that it stems from a passion for the lost and acknowledges the prompting of the Holy Spirit. It is objective in that it can be verified (or discredited) by history, sociological observation and God's Word.

In some instances false assumptions about spiritual mapping have led to superstition and self-deception. In many more they have frightened conservative believers away from a discipline that could be of genuine benefit.

Given this confusion it is worth taking a moment to examine some of the more notable of these misconceptions. By clearly identifying what spiritual mapping isn't, we can better avoid the dual errors of elitist mysticism and blanket rejection.

SPIRITUAL MAPPING IS NOT THE PRODUCTION OF BIZARRE MAPS

At a recent meeting in southern Louisiana an earnest woman presented me with a hand-drawn map of the Mississippi-Missouri River. As I paused to examine her unusual sketch, I noticed that she had attached spiritual significance to every major turn of the 6,000-mile waterway.

As if this were not strange enough, a few weeks later I received a map of England that depicted spiritual strongholds in the shape of various insects. (According to the British intercessor who mailed it to me, the earwig and scorpion were especially significant.)

The worrisome thing is that these maps are not uncommon. Every week I add new exhibits to the already ample stacks that adorn my library table.

Especially popular is the "connect the dots" approach—a technique that links subjectively chosen map coordinates to "reveal" everything from satanic pentagrams to spiritual power corridors.[7] Many of these sinister designs are presented as the demonically inspired handiwork of Masonic city planners. While there is no denying Masonic influence in certain urban layouts, the significance of this influence is sometimes exaggerated.[8]

Despite being touted as authoritative revelation, these maps are nearly always detached from supporting evidence. And it is this detachment, coupled with the tendency of many modern researchers to shrug it off, that betrays a deep confusion over the true nature of spiritual mapping.

~~~

BY BASING THEIR PRODUCTS ON INADEQUATE SURVEYING, THEOLOGICAL DOGMA OR IMAGINATIVE OR WISHFUL THINKING, TODAY'S SPIRITUAL MAPMAKERS ARE REMINISCENT OF MEDIEVAL CARTOGRAPHERS WHO FILLED IN BLANK SPOTS WITH FANCIFUL CREATURES.

~~~

By basing their products on inadequate surveying, theological dogma or imaginative or wishful thinking, today's spiritual mapmakers are reminiscent of medieval cartographers who filled in blank spots with fanciful creatures—a practice that inspired Jonathan Swift's well-known satirical verse:

> So Geographers, in Afric maps,
> With savage-pictures fill their gaps;

And o'er uninhabitable downs
Place elephants for want of towns.[9]

SPIRITUAL MAPPING IS NOT SUBJECTIVE IMAGERY

After concluding a lecture on spiritual mapping in the mid-1990s, I was approached by a woman from California who announced that she had already identified the precise location of the enemy's stronghold in her community. Intrigued, I urged her to elaborate.

"It's in my church," she continued with an air of certainty. "It is centered in a stained-glass window located at the front of our sanctuary. I have offered to pay for the window to be replaced, but my pastor isn't keen on the idea. He is only willing to let me cover it with brown wrapping paper."

This account reveals a flawed assumption about spiritual warfare—namely that problems in the spiritual dimension can simply be covered up. It also illustrates how abstract ideas and mental fantasies are sometimes confused with genuine spiritual mapping.

In a similar case, an American pastor claimed to have discovered a site where demonic powers secretly emanate from the bowels of the earth. After subsequently anointing the location with oil, he announced that the infernal exit had been "cleansed and sealed."

Forgoing paper maps, the authors of such fantasies instead project their imaginations directly onto the canvas of reality. Every day, without a tinge of embarrassment, they assign dubious spiritual meaning to everything from natural elements (rivers, hills and islands) to various forms of architecture (especially public buildings and monuments).

SPIRITUAL MAPPING IS NOT CENTERED ON THE DEMONIC

Another tendency of many spiritual mappers is to give undue, and even exclusive, attention to the demonic. This habit is most often seen in the rush to assign names to territorial spirits or to identify spiritual power corridors known as ley lines.

Although God may well give such revelation, there is no suggestion in Scripture (or recent case studies) that it is a universal
requirement for successful ministry.

Any investigation of the spiritual dynamics at work in a
needy community must consider three fundamental questions:

1. What is wrong with my community?
2. Where did the problem come from?
3. What can be done to change things?

While the first two inquiries often do highlight satanic activity, it is a mistake to equate any answers we may glean with a finished spiritual mapping product. Communities do not change
merely because we have become aware of the nature and origins
of spiritual strongholds; they change because revived believers
enter into fervent and united prayer.

To assess the potential for spiritual breakthroughs we must consider initiatives taken by God and His people. We must ask what the
Church is doing to cultivate an appetite for unity, holiness and
prayer and whether there is evidence the Holy Spirit is responding to
these initiatives. Unless and until we complete this tour of the "light
side" of spiritual mapping, we will not succeed in our mission.

SPIRITUAL MAPPING IS NOT A MAGIC WAND

Other Christians presume—or at least hope—that spiritual mapping is a quick fix for whatever ails their community. It is touted
as a miracle cure, a shortcut to wellness. If one will just do the
"research" (document subjective impressions), breakthroughs
will follow in rapid succession.

This notion is most often found in Western societies where
attention spans are measured in seconds and the work ethic has
been eroded by formulas, gimmicks and gizmos. Unfortunately
for its advocates (wherever they may be), it is false.

Spiritual mapping is neither quick nor magical. Demystified, it is a heavy schedule of hard, disciplined work. Those who are not up to community networking, rigorous research and long hours before God in prayer need not apply.

SPIRITUAL MAPPING IS NOT THE ONLY WAY
Another false assumption is that God cannot move in a community unless local believers have undertaken a rigorous spiritual mapping project. Because the discipline is a contributing factor in many success stories, proponents contend that spiritual mapping must be pursued in every case.

The problem with this argument is that it strips God of His sovereignty. It neglects to consider His extraordinary resourcefulness and originality—attributes that are well documented in the Biblical accounts of Nehemiah (in Jerusalem) and Jonah (in Nineveh).

SPIRITUAL MAPPING IS NEITHER QUICK NOR MAGICAL. THOSE WHO ARE NOT UP TO COMMUNITY NETWORKING, RIGOROUS RESEARCH AND LONG HOURS BEFORE GOD IN PRAYER NEED NOT APPLY.

SPIRITUAL MAPPING IS NOT SPIRITUAL WARFARE
Finally, it is important to point out that while spiritual mapping and spiritual warfare are often mentioned in the same breath, they are actually two distinct activities. Whereas the former is a research discipline that produces intelligence on the spiritual dynamics at work in a given community, the latter is the use to which this intelligence is put (usually fervent prayer, fasting and evangelism).

Spiritual mapping is not a solution, but rather a means to a solution. It involves prayer but only as an aid to the acquisition and interpretation of critical spiritual intelligence. Its solitary goal is to *prepare the way* for effective intercession.

This distinction is not meant to imply mutual exclusivity. If spiritual mapping and spiritual warfare are not identical twins, they are interdependent blood relatives. To paraphrase the apostle Paul, research without works is dead.

NOTES

1. This tally is taken from Nehemiah chapter 3 although a list in chapter 7 suggests there may well have been additional participants.
2. This is not to say that individual actions do not impinge on the community. They do, sometimes quite profoundly. Examples of this are found in the lives of Achan, whose possession of an illicit Babylonian robe caused God's favor to depart from the armies of Israel (see Josh. 7), and Daniel, whose faithfulness in prayer led King Darius to issue a kingdom-wide decree that "people must fear and reverence the God of Daniel" (Dan. 6:26).
3. George Otis, Jr., *The Twilight Labyrinth* (Grand Rapids: Chosen, 1997), pp. 142-149.
4. Ibid., pp. 192, 193.
5. William Robertson Smith, *The Religion of the Semites: The Fundamental Institutions* (New York: Schocken Books, 1889, 1972), pp. 92, 95.
6. This suburb of Guatemala City is located in the area where the Pan American Highway conveys travelers into the National Highlands. Between this busy foothill community and San Lucas Sacatepequez, there is a significant cluster of religious training and worship centers. In addition to Islamic and Hindu groups there is also the cult of William Soto Santiago, a counterfeit healer who claims to be the Son of God.
7. Known as ley lines, these corridors are commonly believed to connect sources of spiritual power and human bondage. While the associations cited by would-be spiritual mappers are often conjured or forced, the doctrine does carry weight in a number of animist cultures.
8. Not all bizarre maps are hand drawn. Alistair Petrie, an Anglican vicar from British Columbia, tells of a group in Vancouver that reportedly discerns spiritual strongholds by throwing darts at a city map!
9. Quoted in John Noble Wilford, *The Mapmakers* (New York: Vintage Books, 1981), p. 14.

༄

OUT OF THE STARTING BLOCKS

Having explored the nature and purpose of spiritual mapping, it is time to examine the practicalities of launching an actual research project. Where, exactly, does one begin? What is the first order of business?

In providing answers to these questions this chapter will focus on two early tasks: setting project parameters (will you investigate an urban neighborhood or a rural county?) and determining the size and composition of your team. These dual actions represent all-important starting blocks in your race to victory.

If you have never done anything like this before, you may be feeling a bit nervous or inadequate. These emotions are common, so don't let them get the better of you. It is impossible to remember every procedure or methodology. Nobody turns in a flawless performance. So don't worry about it! Doing things right is not as important as doing the right things.

DETERMINING THE SIZE OF YOUR TASK

At the outset of your spiritual mapping campaign you will need to determine how much territory you are going to cover—and why. The boundaries you select should be relevant to your ultimate mission (a transformed community) and to known historical, cultural and spiritual realities. They should also be a realistic reflection of available time and manpower.

To insure that your project parameters are truly meaningful, don't be too quick to adopt prevailing civic or political boundaries. Despite their convenience, these dividing lines are often arbitrary inventions that ignore preexisting facts and affiliations.

A good example of this is found in the American Southwest where the Navajo Indian Reservation spills over the borders of three states (Arizona, Utah and New Mexico). Since the Navajo Nation predates these political designations, tribal members pay more attention to boundaries identified by traditional myths.

Similar examples can be seen in the colonial borders of Africa (which frequently bisect ancient tribal homelands), the Pakistani city of Peshawar (whose history and culture is more closely linked to Pashtu cities inside Afghanistan) and the political subdivisions of Central America (which consign the indigenous Maya to four separate nations). In these and many other cases around the world modern political borders are incongruous with underlying cultural and spiritual domains (see chapter 7 to learn about suprastates and city islands).

SPIRITUAL POWERS CONGREGATE IN PLACES AND
CULTURES WHERE THEY ARE WELCOMED. THE
ONLY BORDERS THEY RECOGNIZE ARE THOSE THAT
HAVE BEEN ESTABLISHED THROUGH PACTS
WITH THEIR FOLLOWERS.

Because an important goal of spiritual mapping is to identify these domains, your research campaign should not be sidetracked by artificial demarcations. Spiritual powers congregate in places and cultures where they are welcomed. The only borders they recognize are those that have been established through pacts with their followers.[1]

With this in mind it is a good idea to keep the dimensions of your project flexible. As you learn more about your target area you can adjust boundaries to include or exclude certain districts or neighborhoods. Always remember that your goal is to achieve authentic results, not tidiness.

Good results also demand realism. The dimensions of your project should not exceed the resources at your disposal. If they do, you and your colleagues are likely to end up fruitless and frustrated.

Until now the most effective spiritual mapping campaigns have focused on neighborhoods and small-to-medium-sized towns (although progress has also been reported on university campuses and Indian reservations). Besides being more manageable, undertakings of this size keep the action closer to home—a fact that gives participants an important vested interest.

Projects aimed at cities, counties, states and provinces have been less successful. Overwhelmed by the sheer size and complexity of their targets, many teams have settled for superficial conclusions or abandoned their quest altogether.

While geography is often seen as the reason for such failures, the real nemesis is population density. A block of high-rise apartments in Hong Kong can easily present a greater challenge than an entire county in rural Ireland. Spiritual mapping is about discovering what is going on inside of people's heads; and the more heads you have to study, the more difficult your project becomes.

On average, it will take a competent, part-time team between one and two years to map a large neighborhood or a medium town. If you want to expedite this process, your best move is to increase your project manpower. Cutting back on the quality of your report will only lead to superficial, and possibly dangerous, conclusions.

FORMING STRATEGIC PARTNERSHIPS

If you determine that your research task is too large for a single group (a likely scenario if your objective is to map a large metropolitan area), consider forming a strategic partnership with other local fellowships. This is an excellent way to get a big job done quickly.

As I noted in chapter 4, churches in Cali, Colombia, enjoyed great success with this approach. After defining the parameters of their task (an entire metropolitan area), dozens of neighborhood fellowships proceeded to establish cooperative mapping campaigns in each of the city's 22 administrative districts. When their work was complete, the results were stitched together like panels on a patchwork quilt.

Besides saving time, partnerships of this kind escalate vested interest. Participants are keen not only to learn about their immediate neighborhoods but also to see how their discoveries fit into the larger mosaic of the surrounding community.

The book of Nehemiah reveals that at least 41 Hebrew clans took part in the rebuilding of the walls of Jerusalem.[2] Chapter 3 describes how these people—which included priests, merchants, goldsmiths and perfume makers—served the collective good by taking on tasks located in their own districts and neighborhoods. Rephaiah, ruler of a half district of Jerusalem, restored an area adjoining the goldsmiths and perfume makers (see verse 9), while Nehemiah, ruler of a half-district of Beth Zur, worked "up to a point opposite the tombs of David" (verse 16). Hashabiah, ruler of half the district of Keilah, "carried out repairs for his district" (verse 17), while Jedaiah "made repairs opposite his house" (verse 10).

As a result of this collective effort, the wall was completed in 52 days—an astonishing feat by any standard. Nehemiah reported that "When all our enemies heard about this, all the surrounding nations were afraid and lost their self-confidence" (6:16). On the day of the city's rededication to God, two great choirs led the people on a boisterous praise march around the wall. As they offered great sacrifices, the "sound of rejoicing in Jerusalem could be heard far away" (12:43).

If you decide to forge a strategic partnership in your own city, be sure to allow ample time for participants to reach a prayerful consensus on project objectives and methodologies. Good dialogue up-front will help you avoid unpleasant surprises down the line.

ORGANIZING THE RESEARCH TEAM

One of the first things a successful spiritual mapping team needs is competent leadership. Without it, your project is doomed to flounder on the rocks of confusion and procrastination.

The team leader can be either male or female, but he or she must command the respect and attention of all the other members. The fact that they are adept with facts and figures means nothing if they are inept at social interaction. Such people can make valuable team members, but they are unsuitable for leadership.

Inflated egos, personal agendas and dictatorial personalities should also be avoided. As with all complex activities, spiritual mapping requires a melding of diverse talents and personalities. To achieve this a team leader must be prepared to exercise considerable wisdom, patience and humility.

The best leaders subdivide their talent into working groups that concentrate on distinct tasks like library research, field interviews and intercessory prayer. The first of these groups, often called *the archival unit*, consists of individuals who are skilled at culling information from secondary sources such as books, journals, dissertations and maps. They are most productive in libraries and archives and tend to enjoy surfing the Internet.

The field unit, on the other hand, is made up of people who thrive on social interaction. Their arena of effectiveness is the street where they can extract information from observation and personal interviews. Without their contribution, the spiritual mapping campaign can easily take on an academic, and even aloof, character.

The final group, known as *the intercessory unit*, is comprised of individuals who have learned to appreciate the quiet place of prayer. These disciplined prayer warriors have found there is a treasure-trove of information awaiting those who will faithfully record the promptings and revelations of the Holy Spirit.

In recruiting talent for these various units, it is important to select participants who are committed for the duration of the project—be it 52 days or 24 months. Aside from unexpected intrusions like sickness or hastily assigned business trips, they should not ask to be excused from their spiritual mapping duties. Managing a complex project with a stable team is difficult enough. Once members are allowed to bounce in and out of the action, the task becomes nearly impossible.

CHARACTERISTICS OF A SPIRITUAL MAPPER

While much has been written in recent years about the qualities of an effective counselor, missionary or church administrator, there is virtually no literature on what makes a good spiritual mapper. To help fill this void, I have assembled a list of attributes (both general and specific) gleaned from successful projects around the world.

GENERAL ATTRIBUTES
As you recruit talent for your spiritual mapping team, it is important to note that this practice often attracts loners and misfits. To eliminate these problem candidates without denying useful diversity, you should concentrate on individuals who measure up to the following character standard.

Right Motive
Remember that the motivating force behind all spiritual mapping activity should be a passion for lost souls. People who want to use spiritual mapping to peer

voyeuristically into the basement of their communities are not suitable team members.

Commitment to the Community

Spiritual mapping is not for circuit riders. As pastor Bob Beckett has pointed out, "Territorial revelations are tied to territorial commitments."[3] God wants to know that we mean business before He removes the scales from our eyes. Secrets are both precious and powerful and the Holy Spirit doles them out to those He can trust.

Servant Attitude

Spiritual mappers should be team players. Their ambition is to serve their fellow researchers and the spiritually lost whose circumstances they are investigating. Individuals who are not open and humble and who like to maintain the illusion that they are part of an exclusive "in the know" unit need to be avoided at all costs.

Accountability

People who are eager to poke their noses into the heart of darkness but are unwilling to submit to leadership oversight pose a danger to themselves, their teammates, and possibly the cause of Christ. By chafing at accountability they show they have no appreciation for the warfare dynamics of spiritual mapping. There is no place for Lone Rangers in this business. Accountable team members are covered team members.

OVERLY MYSTICAL RESEARCHERS
(OR INTERCESSORS) CAN PROJECT
IMAGINARY PHANTOMS ONTO
THE CANVAS OF REALITY.
THOSE WHO ARE OVERLY
CONSERVATIVE
ARE LIABLE TO MISS SEEING
THE REAL DRAGONS.

Spiritual Balance

Since Satan is a known liar and deceiver, those who follow his trail must have command of their spiritual equilibrium. Overly mystical researchers (or intercessors) can project imaginary phantoms onto the canvas of reality. Those who are overly conservative are liable to miss seeing the real dragons. The spiritual dimension is a deep and mysterious place. Those who enter it need to know the voice and character of their Guide.

Good Work Habits

The writer of Ecclesiastes admonishes: "Whatever your hand finds to do, do it with all your might" (9:10). Hard work spotlights the character of people. As Sam Ewing quipped in *Reader's Digest*, "Some turn up their sleeves, some turn up their noses, and some don't turn up at all."[4] Like any other worthwhile Kingdom endeavor, spiritual mapping demands diligent, resourceful and honest workers. Those who are always looking for the path of least resistance will fare poorly in this discipline.

SPECIFIC ATTRIBUTES

Spiritual mapping candidates should also display attributes that suit them for service on the team's archival, field or intercessory subunits. The following mini-profiles should give you an idea of what to look for.

Archival Unit

The best participants in this unit are detail-oriented people. From obscure footnotes to historical chronologies, they find beauty in the fine print. They have a penchant for accuracy and nearly always view patience as a virtue. Resourcefulness is also a strong suit. Tell them something doesn't exist or can't be done and you will only light their fire. To them the quest is half the fun. They have excellent memories, good analytical faculties and are generally well-read and computer literate.

Field Unit

Every member of the spiritual mapping field unit should be what is known as a "people person." These individuals are every bit as determined as their archival colleagues, but they like extracting information via their social skills. They are generally articulate (which helps them arrange and conduct interviews), as well as being keen observers and wise judges of character.

Intercessory Unit

The most useful intercessory support personnel are patient and disciplined. They have learned through experience that God is often deliberate in His communications with men. At the same time, they have enough sense to pull out a pen and paper whenever He does start talking. Recognizing the potential for error in their subjective world, mature intercessors spend quality time in God's Word and with His saints. They are often the first of the three subunits to perceive important cautions and patterns.

PROJECT COMMISSIONING

Before you actually send your team onto the streets, it is important to insure that local believers are ready for the fruits of their labor. Remember that the purpose of spiritual mapping is to sustain fervent intercession and pave the way for effective evangelism. If community churches are not yet united in prayer, or if there is no evident passion for the lost, your project may be premature.

Should this be the case in your community, don't force a research campaign. Rather, pray earnestly that God will create an appetite in the hearts of local leaders and laity for unity, prayer and evangelism. Having the best intelligence in the neighborhood is of little value if no one is interested in it.

If, on the other hand, the church in your community is begging for prayer fuel, it is probably time to begin spiritual mapping. In fact, without your efforts, it is unlikely that they will manage to make the transition from the beachhead stage to a full-fledged spiritual breakthrough.

Your next step is to identify a commissioning authority. Like missionaries and church planters, you want to be sent out by a leadership structure that holds expectations for your project and is capable of providing spiritual accountability. If your project is small, this structure can be the pastoral staff or eldership of your local church. If your campaign is part of a community-wide initiative, a ministerial association or other apostolic body can provide the necessary covering.

The commissioning itself should be a public affair. Besides formalizing a kind of "protective custody," it is an opportunity to explain your plan to fellow congregates and solicit their prayer support. The idea is to build healthy anticipation among local pastors, evangelists and intercessors. If your attitude and timing is right, this solemn event should prompt calls for regular progress reports.

To make such a presentation, of course, you must first develop a set of sound research objectives. To do this requires that you know what you are looking for. While the task of identifying intellectual prey may sound easy enough, it is a test that many spiritual mappers fail. For this reason I have made it the sole subject of our next chapter.

NOTES

1. George Otis, Jr., *The Twilight Labyrinth* (Grand Rapids: Chosen, 1997), pp. 136-149, 192-198.
2. This tally is taken from Nehemiah chapter 3 although a list in chapter 7 suggests there may well have been additional participants.
3. Bob Beckett, *Commitment to Conquer* (Grand Rapids: Chosen, 1997), pp. 69, 70.
4. Sam Ewing, *Reader's Digest*, "Quotable Quotes" (November 1996), p. 37.

❧

PEELING BACK THE DARKNESS

Urban navigators routinely rank the city of London, England, among the world's most confounding real estate. In addition to being jigsawed by the Thames river, the British capital presents a nightmarish hodgepodge of one-way streets, roundabouts, dark tunnels and dead ends.

Some 23,000 licensed taxi drivers currently ply these concrete and asphalt arteries in their signature black cabs. If they look like they know where they are going, it is because they have acquired "The Knowledge"—the ability to recognize some 800 routes and 1,400 different places of interest (including memorials, hotels, parks and theaters).

According to *The Baltimore Sun* reporter Bill Glauber, "'The Knowledge' was introduced at the time of the 1851 Great Exhibition, a fair that celebrated Britain's industrial might in the Victorian era. The public wanted the cabdrivers of horse-drawn carriages to know their way around the city.... [in time] 'The Knowledge' became a skill handed down through generations, fathers teaching sons, friends instructing friends."[1]

"The Knowledge" is still a rite of passage today. In order to conquer a series of rigorous oral exams administered by London's Metropolitan Police (the trade has been regulated since the seventeen century), would-be cabdrivers must memorize 792 square miles of roadways and landmarks. The process can take years and requires supreme dedication. In fact, 7 of every 10 who attempt to gain "The Knowledge" fall short of the prize.

A similar level of dedication is required of spiritual mappers, although the dropout rate is statistically higher than that found among London's trainee cabdrivers. In this tough discipline the challenge is not to circumvent traffic jams but to discover and remove obstacles to revival. Our "knowledge" is not just a familiarity with physical milestones and landmarks but an ability to discern and navigate the spiritual dimension.

❧

HAVING BEEN ANIMATED BY THE VERY BREATH OF GOD, WE ARE CAPABLE OF DISCERNING SPIRIT AS WELL AS FLESH. THIS ALLOWS US TO RECOGNIZE THE DELICATE INTERPLAY BETWEEN SPIRITUAL CAUSES AND MATERIAL EFFECTS AND VICE VERSA.

❧

The good news, as I noted in chapter 3, is that human beings are actually well suited for research in two dimensions. Having been animated by the very breath of God (see Gen. 2:7), we are capable of discerning spirit as well as flesh. This allows us to recognize the delicate interplay between spiritual causes and material effects and vice versa.[2]

It is true that many spiritual mappers come up short in their quest for understanding. But this is an indictment not of their ability to see but of their confusion over what to look for. Good research must start with meaningful objectives.

WHAT ARE WE LOOKING FOR?

As you establish research targets for your project, three basic questions should guide your planning:

1. What is wrong with my community?
2. Where did the problem come from?
3. What can be done to change things?

While more sophisticated lists can certainly be developed, they will only be an extrapolation of these root questions.

With a clear set of objectives it is reasonably easy to establish what are known in intelligence circles as *essential mission elements*. These elements represent the practical core of your research assignment. They are the jewels of knowledge that must be brought home for the mission to be considered a success.

A prime example of this concept is found in the account of the Hebrew spies dispatched by Moses into the Promised Land (see Num. 13). Rather than simply encouraging his scouts to go out and learn whatever they could, Moses handed them a set of eight essential mission elements. These included developing intelligence on enemy population and fortifications and bringing back samples of Canaan's fruit.

Spontaneity may add spice to one's love life, but it is a poor approach to research. "In the fields of observation," the famed scientist Louis Pasteur once wrote, "chance only favors the mind prepared."[3] Good results are an effect caused by good prior planning.

DISTILLING RESEARCH OBJECTIVES INTO QUESTIONS

If the first step in collecting relevant information involves knowing one's objectives, then the second step is remembering those objectives! To paraphrase Proverbs 29:18: Where there is no objective, the people wander.

To keep your mission objectives in mind, it is useful to translate them into practical exploratory questions (see "Discovery Questions" in appendix 1). This helps to clarify your thinking, and also expedites your journey.

As you develop your investigative notebook, bear in mind that the most powerful inquiries begin with the words *What, Why* and *How.* These interrogatives are like a collection of specialized keys that open the doors to knowledge, to understanding, and to wisdom.

Successful spiritual mappers will use all of these questions. Knowing *what* the spiritual strongholds are in your community is not the same as understanding *why* they are there or *how* to get rid of them.

Once you have decided on the wording of your questions, it is a good idea to categorize them according to your basic mission objectives. These objectives can be expressed either in terms of the core questions mentioned at the beginning of this section or through the expanded research categories listed below. Both approaches have their advocates, although most people find the latter to be more useful when it comes to laying out a final report.

Primary Research Categories

1. The Status of Christianity
   Relates to Core Question #1: What is wrong with my community?
2. Prevailing Social Bondages
   Relates to Core Question #1: What is wrong with my community?
3. Worldviews and Allegiances
   Relates to Core Question #1: What is wrong with my community?
4. Spiritual Opposition
   Relates to Core Question #1: What is wrong with my community?
5. The Evolution of Current Circumstances
   Relates to Core Question #2: Where did the problem come from?
6. The Potential for Spiritual Breakthroughs
   Relates to Core Question #3: What can be done to change things?

The following pages will help you construct specific questions for each of these mini-investigations. Read the category descriptions carefully before building your lines of inquiry.

THE STATUS OF CHRISTIANITY

The first thing you want to know about your community is the extent to which the gospel has taken root. Is your town an evangelist's graveyard or part of a "Bible Belt"? How many Christians worship in the area? What percentage of the population do they represent?

A second set of questions relates to the nature of Christianity in your neighborhood. Are old revival fires still burning or has the fervor of previous years given way to a liberal, lukewarm religion? Are local churches predominantly Protestant or Roman Catholic? Do they show an interest in presenting the gospel to nonbelievers? What is the status of current evangelistic initiatives?

Another matter you will want to examine concerns the community's perception of organized Christianity. Do people see the church as a relevant force or an outmoded institution? Have scandals diminished the church's reputation? What kind of public activities (marches, picketing, food distribution) do Christians participate in?

In gathering answers to these questions you will need to strike a balance between sensitivity and candor. While you don't want to come across as judgmental of your fellow parishioners, you also want to avoid viewing the world through rose-colored glasses. Take your time, for the knowledge you gain on these topics will serve as an important contextual backdrop for the balance of your study.

PREVAILING SOCIAL BONDAGES

Another important research assignment involves gathering outward evidence of spiritual darkness in the community. You are not trying to prove that this darkness exists—you are presumably already convinced it does. Rather, your mission is to identify specific forms and haunts favored by prevailing deceptive powers.

Your first task is to catalog conditions of pain—things like injustice, poverty, violence and disease. You want to know how widespread these problems are and how long they have been around.

It is also important to assess the nature and prevalence of destructive vices. These corrosive activities include such things as intoxication, gambling and sexual immorality (pornography and prostitution). They differ from the above-mentioned conditions of pain in that their wounds are largely self-inflicted.

A third area of research concerns the disintegration of stabilizing social values and structures. Key symptoms to look for are corruption and divorce. When they are prevalent in a community, it is a sure sign that government, business and family life is unraveling.

To identify other troubling trends you will need to formulate questions like: What new forms is sin taking in the community? Is there a new militancy on the part of sinners? What, if any, role does the media have in promoting spiritual darkness in the community?

The answers you glean from these inquiries will provide a useful, if sobering, overview of the enemy's handiwork in your city.

WORLDVIEWS AND ALLEGIANCES

Having investigated the status of Christianity and prevailing social bondages, your next step is to identify important underlying ideologies. These are the mind-sets and allegiances that make the community tick.

In addition to cataloging the predominant religious and secular philosophies (such as Buddhism, Judaism, rationalism and animism), you also want to track significant events and practices associated with these philosophies. How exactly do people show their devotion? Is this merely a cultural reflex, or is there evidence that people are genuinely serious about their beliefs?

It is also important to note any reaffirmations of ancient spiritual pacts or practices. These validations can take the form of political resolutions, "heritage" recovery or religious festivals and pilgrimages.

Lastly, you will need to discover the identities of any influential ideological leaders, role models, idols or deities. To whom or to what do people in the community give their allegiance? The answer may lead you to human beings (gurus, politicians or entertainers) or to demonic or mythical personalities (Buddha, Shiva or the Hopi kachinas).

SPIRITUAL OPPOSITION

To fully appreciate why evangelism and Church growth are hindered in your community you will also need to explore the matter of spiritual opposition. You want to know where the resistance is coming from and, if it is not readily apparent, what form it is taking.

⊗

INVENTING TERRITORIAL SPIRITS OR
EMBELLISHING THEIR ROLE CAN LEAD TO
SERIOUS DECEPTION (SEE JER. 23:16,27).

⊗

On the question of *who* is hindering the gospel, your investigation should take into account two possible sources: human groups and personalities (militant homosexuals, occultists, traditional religious leaders), and prevailing territorial spirits. The latter can exercise their influence through human agents (Jezebel, Herod, Nero) or through deities and idols that have been adopted by particular segments of the community (see Psalm 106:36-38).

It is important not to force things here. Inventing territorial spirits or embellishing their role can lead to serious deception (see Jer. 23:16,27). If there are connections that God wants you to note, He will bring them to your attention. At the same time, you must not lose sight of the enemy's versatility or evil ambition. The Scriptures portray him as a master manipulator whose touch can affect nations (see Dan. 10), city councils (see 1 Thess. 2:18), rioting mobs (see John 8:44,59) and even natural elements (see Mark 4:39).

In documenting the various forms that spiritual opposition is taking in your community, be on the lookout for such things as witchcraft, anti-Christian legislation, economic discrimination, public mockery and physical persecution. These things are real and on the rise.

THE EVOLUTION OF CURRENT CIRCUMSTANCES

Before you can establish an effective evangelistic and/or intercessory action plan, you must first try to understand why things are the way they are. How has your community come to be what it is today? What do you know about the origin of contemporary hindrances to the gospel?

To answer these questions it is necessary to examine the historical and spiritual roots of your area. Who were the original peoples? What factors or motives led them to found a permanent community?

You will also want to investigate significant confluent events like natural disasters, military invasions and the influx of new religions (see chapter 7). How did these occurrences alter the life and identity of the community? Did the inhabitants of the time attempt to resolve traumatic circumstances by entering into pacts with the spirit world? Did their actions compound or modify earlier arrangements?

As you look for answers to these questions, bear in mind that every generation tends to view itself as detached from the continuum of history. Communities do the same thing. This nearsightedness often leads people to miss important historical connections—connections that can help explain why things are the way they are.

Spiritual mapping, like a good pair of glasses, offers a remedy for this problem. Once we see just how linked we are to the motives, pacts and events that have preceded us, we can employ repentance and reconciliation to shatter long-standing bondages.

THE POTENTIAL FOR SPIRITUAL BREAKTHROUGHS

Your final task is to ascertain the potential for spiritual change within the community. In fulfilling this mission you are looking not so much for historical facts as for hopeful signs. Has the church positioned itself for action by cultivating unity, holiness and prayer? Do large-scale prayer meetings and/or social reconciliation efforts suggest an imminent spiritual breakthrough? Is there a sense of hopeful expectancy among believers?

Another barometer of spiritual health is the quality of community intercession. Are local prayer warriors aware of the facts and challenges you have uncovered in your research? Are they begging for added intelligence to stoke their intercessory fervor? If the answer to both of these questions is "yes," you can expect great things to come.

And don't forget to look for evidence that God may already have begun to break up strongholds in your neighborhood. If you can document large-scale conversions, social reconciliation and/or public miracles, chances are high that the Holy Spirit has indeed arrived on the scene. Dramatic political or social wind shifts are also worthy of attention, as are indications of economic or other forms of judgment.

Now that you have a better idea of the kind of information you will be looking for, it is time to move on to a more thorough discussion of spiritual mapping targets and techniques. In the coming pages you will learn how to work with data sets, how to identify sources of spiritual influence, and how to develop historical timelines. If you go on to apply these teachings, you will soon become a master at layering space and weaving time.

NOTES

1. Bill Glauber, "Seeking 'Knowledge' in London" *The Baltimore Sun* (November 19, 1997), p. 2A.

2. Many Christians, particularly in the busy West, choose to ignore all but the spiritual dimension's most cosmic features (heaven, hell, God, the devil), while others tend to project features out of their imaginations. Both of these tendencies are serious errors. Whereas the former ignores what *is* there, the latter is entranced by what *is not* there. In both cases, the works of the devil remain cloaked and the kingdom of darkness flourishes.

3. Louis Pasteur, address given on the inauguration of the Faculty of Science, University of Lille (December 7, 1854).

⟨❧⟩

LAYERING SPACE AND WEAVING TIME

Acclaimed author Scott Russell Sanders tells how his father, on coming to a new place, would take a pinch of dirt and taste it like a well-bred wine connoisseur. Asked why he did this, the old man replied, "Just trying to figure out where I am." Watching his father repeat this ritual some years later, Sanders asked him if he had ever been lost. "No," he answered, "but there's been a few times when I didn't know where anything else was."[1]

As human beings we need reference points to survive. The more important of these markers define our position relative to larger, and sometimes hidden, physical realities. Airport beacons bring us down to earth in a safe place. Road signs tell us what highway we are on or that the bridge ahead has been washed out. Barbed-wire fences warn that we have approached a territory that should not be intruded upon.

Maps are perhaps the most useful reference tool of all. In their book *The Nature of Maps,* Arthur H. Robinson and Barbara Bartz Petchenik argue that "the concept of spatial relatedness...is a quality without which it is difficult or impossible for the human mind to apprehend anything."[2] If we cannot orient ourselves within our environment, we will be lost—and not just physically.

Robinson and Petchenik define a map as "a graphic representation of the milieu." This definition, though simple, is also powerful. By not restraining itself to earthly terrain, it allows us to apply the benefits of mapmaking to other equally important environments and settings. (Examples of this are seen in recent efforts to map the human brain and DNA.)[3]

Nor does spiritual mapping confine itself to geography alone. As we noted in the previous chapter, it is a discipline that is equally concerned with history. Since clues to our current circumstances are strewn across both time and space, we must investigate events as well as places.

In the following pages I will introduce several concepts and tools that can help you better evaluate the spiritual dynamics at work in your community. Some of these will enable you to make important connections by visualizing information in different combinations. Others are designed to help you understand how communities are influenced and how they change over time.

COMMUNITIES ARE LIKE RIVERS

"Riverness," which Sanders defines as "the appeal of a river, the way it speaks to us," has to do with our need for a sense of direction as we navigate the complex terrain of life. Some aspects of human endeavor, such as relationships and communities, are so complicated that we instinctively reach for analogies and metaphors to sort them out. It is our way of maintaining an inner order.

Like rivers, communities start small. Their modest origins are like a melting mountain snowpack that is channeled downhill in the form of rivulets, streams and waterfalls. In the formative stages, these infant communities can tumble and swirl for months, or even years, before assuming a distinct identity. In time, however, these communities-to-be will merge with other influential streams, their flow picking up girth and momentum.

During a community's journey to respectability or infamy its ever-changing course is affected by a series of significant internal and external influences. In keeping with the river metaphor, I have called these stimuli *confluent events* and *contouring events*. The former is an influence that flows into the community from the outside, while the latter represents the flow of the community itself. Cultural geographers study the impact of these events.

CONFLUENT EVENTS

In America's heartland the undulating Ohio River serves as the boundary between five states. Before it empties into the Mississippi at Cairo, Illinois, well over 1,000 miles from its headwaters, it is modified by dozens of tributaries, including the Muskingum, Cumberland, Scioto, Kentucky, Green, Wabash, Kanawha, Tennessee, White Oak, Big Sandy and Great Miami. Downstream from each confluence the river reveals whatever substance—be it factory effluence, alluvial silt or winter ice—the tributary has injected into its vein. The effect, as Sanders records with literary brilliance, can be dramatic.

> Depending on the light, the season, and the stage of the river, the water can remind you of coffee with cream, the amber of tobacco juice, the green of moss, the lavender of lilacs, or robin's egg blue; or the surface can become a liquid mirror, doubling the islands and hills.[4]

Swimming in the Ohio, which Sanders calls "the concentrated waters of a hundred streams," he tries to "feel all the remotest creeks of that vast basin trickling through [him]."[5] It is a profound and rewarding experience.

The routine can also work for those who take thoughtful walks through their community. The primary difference is that social currents are formed not by rushing waters but by the course of history. Communities, like rivers, are affected by the inflow of external influences. These tributaries can include wars, migrations, natural disasters or new state laws. They can also include the arrival of the gospel or a competing ideology. Over time, these confluent events will play a major role in defining the life and character of the community.

CONTOURING EVENTS

It is a mistake, however, to assume that communities, or rivers, are inherently passive subjects. Both have an active, even aggressive, dimension that cannot be ignored. Just as a river wears a groove in the earth as it slides within its banks, so the flow of a community has a profound impact on the historical landscape.

This flow is not generated by external, or confluent, forces alone. It is also the product of internal events like town meetings and local elections. Moral and spiritual choices—such as the decision to receive or reject the gospel—also factor in.

Actions taken to preserve a deceptive tradition also qualify as contouring events. In ancient Babylon, for example, it was common for kings to rebuild temples dedicated to one or another of their many gods. To do this, excavations had to be made to uncover ancient foundation platforms, the original divinely approved pattern of the temple. This was followed by a ceremonial purification of the site, an activity that typically involved the whole town.[6]

To witness the effect of a contouring or confluent event requires patience. It can take months, even years, before the full consequences of a migration or an election become manifest. This deferral of results is similar to the experience of the farmer who has just sown his seed or the child whose teeth have just been fitted with new braces.

The combined effect of these events takes even longer to see. Here we are talking not about a single, near-term episode, but a lifetime of influences. To capture this bigger picture, observers need to take "character snapshots" of the community—preferably within one year of each confluent or contouring event—and place them on a timeline. Viewed collectively, these interim assessments of the community's goals and values reveal the formative impact of key historical events.

The Flow of Communities

Figure 7.1

Place this collection of character snapshots in motion (see Figure 7.1), à la time-lapse photography, and the community becomes a living entity. It is conceived out of vision or avarice, born in a spirit of hope and raised in an environment of mixed influences. Like a developing human life, its identity is forged in pivotal crises and distinct rites of passage. Good choices are rewarded with health and blessing, while poor ones lead to moral, physical and social decay.

❧

THE LIFELINE OF A TOWN WILL PRESENT A DIRECT TRAJECTORY TO HEAVEN OR HELL. BUT WHATEVER ITS ROUTE OR PACE MIGHT BE, THE COMMUNITY—*EVERY* COMMUNITY—IS FLOWING SOMEWHERE. AND THIS FLOW IS THE EFFECT OF OBSERVABLE CAUSES.

❧

In a few instances, the lifeline of a town will present a direct trajectory to heaven or hell. More often, it will vacillate between these destinies like the loops of a lazy river. (The city of Jerusalem offers a striking case in point.) But whatever its route or pace might be, the community—*every* community—is flowing somewhere. And this flow is the effect of observable causes.

YESTERDAY'S SECRETS: THE ROLE
OF CULTURAL GEOGRAPHY

In his book, *Study Out the Land,* author T. K. Whipple observes that our modern community

> lies at the end of the wilderness road, and our past is not a dead past, but still lives in us. Our forefathers had civilization inside themselves, the wild outside. We live in the civilization they created, but within us the wilderness still lingers. What they dreamed, we live. What they lived, we dream.[7]

While Christian conservatives are sometimes leery of those who link present realities to the attitudes and actions of previous generations, the practice does not originate with spiritual warfare proponents. The distinction belongs to a branch of academic research known as cultural geography. Those who embrace its rigors are just as likely to be found in the halls of prestigious universities as on local spiritual mapping teams.

Cultural geographers use timelines and other devices to reveal how various influences are woven together to form distinct cultures and communities. This accentuates the continuum that links the past to the present and helps us see how earlier events help shape modern realities.[8] (I will have more to say about this in the next section.)

Despite the distinctiveness of each age, historian Edward Shils notes that, "No generation, not even those living in this present time of unprecedented dissolution of tradition, creates its own beliefs, patterns of conduct, and institutions."[9] Unfortunately, every generation (and every community) tends to view itself as detached from the continuum of history, and the net effect of this nearsightedness is a creeping, and often fatal, self-deception.

Cultural geography (and anthropology) also concerns itself with the emergence and power of collective knowledge. In *The Old Ways*, author Gary Snyder notes that this knowledge is often related to specific environments. People who dwell on steep jungle slopes, coral atolls or barren arctic deserts, evolve a *spirit of what it is to be there*. This spirit, according to Snyder, speaks of "a direct sense of relation to the 'land.'"[10]

Scott Russell Sanders adds that this knowledge "does not come all at once, but accumulates bit by bit over generations, each person adding to the common lore."[11] In Africa and other parts of the world it is believed that social time—history experienced by the group—amasses power.[12] This power is more than superstitious tradition. It is the product of thousands of people bringing their faith to specific points of contact (these may be ideas, seasons, rituals or places). The longer this process continues, the more it attracts, and is reinforced by, deceptive demonic agents.

History is not a collection of accidents that pop out of a social vacuum. Just as there is a sense and cadence to the universe, so is there a rhyme and reason to our communities. To discern this rhythm, however, we must listen to the entire concerto of our history, not merely the latest stanza.

MULTIDIMENSIONAL DATA PUZZLES

Complex entities can be difficult to apprehend and interpret. To overcome this problem, meteorologists, architects and aircraft design engineers rely on expensive computer modeling programs that allow them to view information in various combinations and from different angles.

Although cities are no less complicated than weather systems or airliners, their secrets can be probed with considerable economy through the use of *data overlays*, which help you visualize places, and *timelines*, which help you keep track of events.

WORKING WITH DATA OVERLAYS

The technique is actually quite simple. You begin by purchasing or creating a base map of your town or neighborhood. This map should be as uncluttered as possible, displaying little more than primary boundaries, landmarks and thoroughfares.

Your next step is to transfer data that can be depicted geographically (sites versus attitudes) onto sheets of clear acetate (obtainable at any stationery or graphics supply store). Each data point, be it a community crime scene or a metaphysical bookstore, can be positioned accurately by placing the acetate sheet on top of your city base map. The resulting product is called a *data set*. What began as a list of addresses or statistical charts now resembles a constellation of stars.

Once you have created a stack of several data sets the fun really starts. By superimposing two or more of these displays on your base map you can often identify meaningful relationships between select facts and issues.

Say, for example, that you lay down a data set depicting the location of evangelical churches in your community (see Figure 7.2). As you study the results for a moment, you notice that a large sector of the community is devoid of churches. The immediate question is, Why? Is it because the area is resistant to the gospel or because no one has attempted to plant a church there?

Data Set A: Evangelical Churches

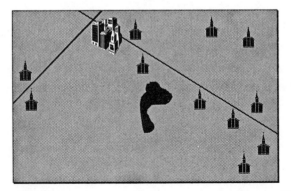

Figure 7.2

Data Set B: Alternative Religious Sites

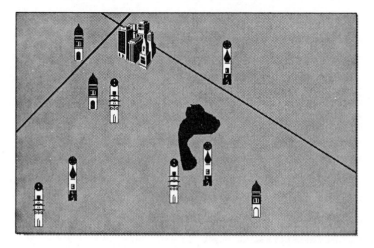

Figure 7.3

To gain additional insight into the situation you can super-impose a second data set, this one revealing the location of local New Age centers. (These could just as well be Buddhist temples, Mormon stakes, or Islamic mosques.) Are these deceptive centers clustered in the area that is lacking evangelical churches? If so, what conclusions might you draw from this? (See figure 7.3.)

Other data sets might reveal a link between commercial sex centers (strip clubs and adult bookstores) and domestic violence.[13] This would alert you to the fact that sin was metasta-sizing in the community and that an important stabilizing influence (the family) was being eroded. It would also give you a good idea as to where these problems were concentrated.

WORKING WITH TIMELINES

Another tool for displaying data is the *timeline*. Unlike maps, which provide spatial orientation, timelines help you keep track of events. The emphasis is on sequence, not distance.

Your first step in creating a timeline is to draw a thick stripe (also known as a stem or stem line) across a horizontally orient-ed piece of paper (landscape mode on a computer). This stem line can be as plain or fancy as you wish. The only requirement is that it be wide enough to contain a descriptive label.

Since timelines can track periods ranging from a single day to thousands of years, the verbiage on respective labels will vary. One document might read "Week 28," while another is titled "August 1999" or "1850-1900."[14]

Once you have finished constructing your stem-line, you are ready to register important events or milestones. Examples might include the founding of your city, the arrival of influential immigrants, or special seasons of revival. You can assign these events to the community chronology by inserting markers in the appropriate places and linking them to brief descriptions or definitions. The markers can be vertical hash marks or unique symbols.

Sample Timeline

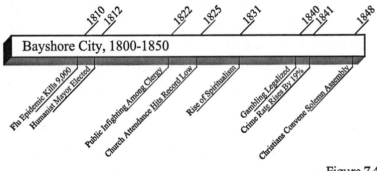

Figure 7.4

As you examine the timeline shown in Figure 7.4, note the cause and effect relationship between various events. In 1810, for example, 9,000 Bayshore City residents succumb to an influenza epidemic. (Additional research reveals this to be 30 percent of the town's population!) The psycho-spiritual impact of this confluent event shows up in the results of a mayoral election two years later. Having determined that God is either unable or unwilling to help in time of crisis, a majority of the community's citizenry decides they must solve their own problems. Their first act is to elect an avowedly humanist mayor.

A decade later the city's pastors allow their frustration with public reaction to the influenza outbreak to degenerate into public infighting. This takes church attendance in Bayshore City to an all-time low. Although the public's hunger for spirituality returns in 1831, Christianity is widely viewed as an empty plate. Many people, searching for an alternative, turn to Spiritualism.

Another important sequence of events occurs during the 1840s. It begins when the city electorate, still looking for diversions, votes to legalize gambling. This action leads to a predictable, and precipitous, rise in the crime rate. By 1848 the moral fabric of the community is torn so severely that Christian leaders convene a solemn assembly.

Bayshore City is but one example of a select chronology. In reality, there is no limit to the number of timelines you can make or, assuming you have a large enough sheet of paper to the number of events they register. Single, large-scale timelines are useful for acquiring perspective and detecting general patterns and trends. Timelines that focus on specific years or decades allow you to zoom in on important details.

You can also develop thematic chronologies. These might track community responses to trauma or adaptive deceptions that have sustained dynasties of spiritual darkness. These potent devices act like special filters that permit you to take an uncluttered look at the forces at work in your area.

In short, timelines reveal how various influences are woven together to form distinct cultures and communities. They highlight the continuum that links the past to the present and demonstrate how the attitudes and actions of previous generations can have a profound effect on the present day. If they are studied carefully, they can also help you reach accurate conclusions about the future.

SUPRASTATES AND CITY ISLANDS

Successful spiritual mapping also requires that a community be viewed in context. Adopting a perspective that is too broad, or too narrow, can cause you to lose sight of important connections. Communities are exceedingly complex and for this reason must be evaluated with great thoroughness and patience.

In addition to discerning the ideological roots of your town or neighborhood you also want to discover where contemporary influences are coming from. This information will allow you to pinpoint specific problems and develop an effective intercessory battle plan.

Two observational concepts are of particular relevance here: *suprastates* and *city islands*. The former helps to expand perspectives that are too narrow, whereas the latter serves as a remedy for viewpoints that are too broad.

SUPRASTATES

When the prefix *supra*, meaning "greater than," is attached to geographic designations like states, provinces or nations, it generally identifies an area of expanded size and common features or interests. These commonalties may be historical, cultural, economic or religious in nature. The existence and use of the term is an acknowledgment that conventional geopolitical boundaries are not always the best way to define reality.

Unfortunately, many spiritual mappers find it difficult to break their preoccupation with modern borders. They like the convenience these familiar boundaries offer and are scarcely bothered that they are often arbitrary and recent inventions. Content with this cramped viewpoint, mappers lose sight of broader historical realities that help form the spiritual bedrock underlying their community.

In Europe, these realities include spiritual pacts forged by Celtic tribes that once roamed the vast distances between Spain and Scotland. In Mesoamerica, territorial covenants initiated by Mayan kings and priests are still active in towns scattered throughout the modern states of Mexico, Belize, Honduras and Guatemala. In the Asian Himalayas, the Arabian Peninsula and the Andean Altiplano, common spiritual histories underlie bondages that extend across dozens of national and provincial borders.

As noted in chapter 5, the United States also has its share of suprastates. Notable examples include the Navajo Nation (see Figure 7.5) whose boundaries have more to do with traditional mythology than modern politics, the Mormon empire whose core constituency is spread out over six states, and Appalachia whose early Celtic immigrants forged a distinct identity in the mountain hollows of West Virginia, Kentucky and Tennessee. A similar affinity prevails in much of New England.

American Suprastates

Figure 7.5

To ignore these extended cultures and the historic seedbeds that produced them is to risk misinterpreting reality. Local strongholds must be viewed in context. As you adjust your perspective, remember that some root systems run laterally.

CITY ISLANDS

Another common error among spiritual mappers is adopting a perspective that is too broad. While context is important, researchers should not *automatically* assume that their community is tethered, historically or otherwise, to surrounding cultures.

Sometimes root systems do strange things. The tropical Banyan tree, for instance, has aerial roots that descend from its branches. Searching for the right soil and air conditions, these roots will often put down some distance away from the main trunk. This creates the illusion that you are looking at an entirely separate tree.

Modern cities behave in the same way. Their geographic footprint is in one culture while their organic connection is somewhere else. Impacted by expanding global networks and large-scale migrations, their citizens often have more in common with colleagues in distant communities than with near neighbors.

In America, the community of Huntsville, Alabama, is located in a state that is often associated with a rural economy and non-progressive or "redneck" political views. The town itself, however, is nicknamed "Space City," and its intimate attachment to the U.S. aerospace industry has caused some to view the city as an urban island set in an alien cultural sea. Instead of discussing soybeans and tobacco, its thousands of workers spend their day exchanging electronic data with leading-edge scientific firms in Houston, Texas; Cape Canaveral, Florida; and California's Silicon Valley.

It is a scenario that plays just as well in Toronto, Tokyo or Tel Aviv. Wired to the world, the citizens of these metropolises today march to ideological drumbeats that are pounded out oceans away—often on computer keyboards. The point of origin may be Paris, New York or Hollywood. But wherever it begins, the distance the message or influence travels is not the issue. It is, rather, how it arrives.

In today's electronic age ideological influences tend to bypass traditional city gates—a fact that is often overlooked by contem-

porary spiritual mappers. While giving due diligence to the cataloging of ports, bridges and highways, many researchers fail to
note that modern lines of influence are increasingly made of
copper or optical fiber.

Throughout the world computer-mediated communications
(CMC) are changing our concept of community, and even of reality. According to technology maven Howard Rheingold,
"Millions of people on every continent [now] participate in computer-mediated social groups known as virtual communities, and
this population is growing fast."[15] The gathering place for these
groups is a conceptual electronic realm known as cyberspace, or
simply "The Net"—the latter being an abbreviated allusion to the
vast network of computers that serves as the technical foundation for CMC.

This "new kind of social habitation," as Rheingold puts it, is
typically experienced through electronic newsgroups and mailing
lists, Internet chat rooms and channels, or Multi-User-Dungeons
(on-line role-playing games popularly known as MUDs). Virtual
communities form when participants coalesce around a particular interest. These interests can include witchcraft, gardening,
astronomy, Communism, auto repair, child rearing, hallucino-
genic drugs, basketball, graphic design, homosexuality, world
missions and countless other themes.

Experience has shown that interaction with group members
often becomes the most anticipated, and the most influential,
event of the day. In his 1993 book, *The Virtual Community:
Homesteading on the Electronic Frontier*, Rheingold concludes: "To
the millions who have been drawn into it, the richness and vital-
ity of computer-linked cultures is attractive, even addictive."[16]

So where are the electronic gateways in your community?
And where do they lead? Who and what is influencing the minds
of your neighbors? When it comes time to look for answers, just
remember that the search may lead your team farther from home
than anyone expected.

To complicate matters further, electronic networking is not the only factor responsible for the emergence of city islands. Large-scale migrations, born of political instability and improved international air transportation, have played an equal role.

Neighborhoods in Vancouver, Canada, having experienced a heavy influx of Chinese immigrants in the late 1990s, now have more in common with Hong Kong than British Colombia. Similar links exist between communities in London and Pakistan, New York and Haiti, Stockholm and Turkey, Los Angeles and Central America, Riyadh and the Philippines, and Paris and North Africa.

In a great many instances, newly arrived immigrants maintain strong ties with their home culture and religion. Chinese settlers in Canada and Britain bring their devotion to kitchen gods and ancestral spirits. Haitian immigrants in New York and Miami set up voodoo altars to appease ancient *loa* (animating spirits). South Asians living in Malaysia and Fiji honor Hindu deities in festivals that are every bit as elaborate as those witnessed in India or Nepal.

As I said at the outset of this section, it is very important that you view your community in context. Without this enhanced perspective you are likely to miss meaningful connections, and missed connections have a way of leading to frustration and even deception.

The name of the game in spiritual mapping is understanding. You want to see things the way God sees them—in context and free of artificial clutter. Character maps, which we discussed in chapter 4, are an important part of this process. So, too, are the contextual filters known as city islands and supra states.

DISCERNING THE LEY OF THE LAND

It should come as no surprise that spiritual mapping also involves investigating locations that have, for one reason or another, emerged as centers of idolatry and demonic attention. This firsthand observation allows you to acquire valuable insight into religious allegiances and possible sources of spiritual opposition. Armed with this intelligence you can proceed to strip the enemy of his cover.

Some people believe power corridors known as *leys,* or *ley lines* connect these dark spiritual sites.[17] Depending on whom you talk to, these lines are either the boundaries of supernatural habitats or patterns of invisible earth energy. Points where these paths intersect are said to be prone to anomalies such as earth lights,[18] haunting phenomena and UFO sightings.

Ley lines were first identified by name in 1925 when Alfred Watkins, an English beer salesman and amateur antiquarian, published his research and theory in his book, *The Old Straight Track.* According to Watkins, leys were "old straight tracks" which crossed the landscape of prehistoric Britain. They were first recognized by ancient men, called Dodmen surveyors, who proceeded to map out the tracks and alignments for trade routes, astronomical sites and holy sites. Watkins said that the alignments followed natural horizon features such as mountain peaks or led to other sacred locations.[19]

Symbolic alignment has also been a central theme of Freemasonry, and it is worth noting that Masons laid out many of the great cities of Europe and the Americas (including Washington, D.C.).[20] According to their beliefs, derived largely from ancient Babylon and Egypt, cities and sacred sites should be properly aligned with the sun's rising in the east (see Ezek. 8:16). Important thoroughfares are typically established in the form of Masonic symbols such as the square and compass.[21]

In East Asia, ley lines are an integral feature of the ancient and widespread practice of *feng shui* (pronounced "fung schway"), a discipline that seeks to promote human health and prosperity by placing cities, office buildings, and homes into harmonious alignment with hidden spiritual forces.

Collectively these terms and practices are part of a quasi-science known as geomancy. Extremely popular in places like Native America, India, and the Orient, geomancy provides a theoretical or doctrinal context for ideas relating to man's alignment to sacred space and spiritual forces. It allows for the creation of a *faithscape* where the dynamics of hallowed space and auspicious timing coalesce to help man realize his identity in the cosmos.[22]

Whatever we may think of ley lines or the power sites they are said to connect, it is impossible, or foolish, to ignore the profound influence they exercise over certain communities. One has only to note the fortunes spent on geomantic architecture in Hong Kong, Singapore and Taipei to appreciate that this is serious business. The same could be said for the untold hours Hindus devote to plotting out pilgrimage routes and shrine locations.

Even more disturbing is the hold this concept has on the indigenous cultures of the northern Andes. Beginning with the Incas, who personified and revered the dramatic landscape that surrounded them, the Indians of the Altiplano have ordered their lives to suit the whims of deities associated with mountains, weather and the sea. To this day, sacrificial ritual sites serve as points of contact with these perceived power sources.[23]

Many Andean mountains belong to a category of supergods called *tius* or *tiós* (uncles), and it is very important to have sight lines from one sacred peak to another.[24] Spiritual power is transferred along these leys, and any visual breach can lead to severe problems. Mountain deities are also related to each other and must be jointly visible to offer their full support.[25]

Some Indians distinguish their communities according to the mountain on which, or near which, they are located. The Qollahuayas, for example, view their sacred homeland along the Peru-Bolivian border as a massive divine body that connects a multitude of villages and spiritual forces.[26] Each year, the various communities (which speak different languages and represent different limbs and organs) come together in a ritual to recreate the mountain's body. The deity's mouth—a place called *Wayra Wisqhani* or "Door of the Wind"—is a cavity within the earth from which air arises. Whenever it rains too much, mountain ritualists feed a llama heart into Wayra Wisqhani so that its breath will blow the clouds away.[27]

Irish (or Celtic) traditionalists also believe in "spirit holes," although in their enchanted world these dimensional gateways appear as small openings in fences, walls or hedgerows. To find these sacred portals the initiated simply follow power-laden "nature spirit" paths.[28]

The scene is much the same in North America where, in the words of Indian shaman Medicine Grizzlybear Lake, "...traditional Native people believe that certain power centers are actually doorways to other dimensions."[29] These sites often include caves, rock outcroppings or designated mounds, and they are used for vision quests or to acquire or redirect power.

According to Lake, some power centers serve as "the residences of special spirit beings who are high in status," while others represent the abode of a particular family of spirits. These territorial spirits are viewed as being the creators, and sometimes the guardians, of sacred power sites.[30] Lake warns, "People who intend to approach and utilize a specific power center [must] prepare themselves properly." In traditional Native American cultures this means "making an invocation to the spirit of the power center" and requesting permission to enter its domain.[31]

What are we to make of such ideas? Are ley lines and spiritual power points real or merely the product of fertile and unredeemed imaginations?

The answer to this dual question seems to be yes and yes. Many traditional beliefs and practices are laced with superstition. But as the horrors of Carthage, the Aztecs and the Nazis remind us, when beliefs are acted upon—even when they are false—there are consequences in the real world.

Sacred power sites represent a system of knowing and acknowledging unseen forces. And as I observed in *The Twilight Labyrinth:*

The Enemy...knows that subjective illusions, if they are to remain effective, must be set up or given credibility by objective realities. Spirits (or ancestors) must occasionally be observable; idols must hear and deliver; astrological predictions must sometimes come to pass. To help him meet these objective expectations, he relies on a vast army of demonic agents capable of oscillating between the spiritual and material dimensions.[32]

As to why people tend to experience only their own cultural spirits, I can answer only that the devil knows to stay in character. He inhabits the script he has been given (or has inspired). He assumes the characteristics we expect. His sole intent, achieved through deceptive, behind-the-scenes manipulation, is to make the fantasy credible.[33]

~&~

LEY LINES ARE NOT THE CENTRAL
FOCUS OF SPIRITUAL MAPPING BUT THEIR PRESENCE
(OR PERCEIVED PRESENCE) IN A COMMUNITY
CAN SUGGEST AN IMPORTANT POINT OF
CONTACT WITH THE SPIRIT WORLD.

~&~

Alistair Petrie, an Anglican vicar and noted authority on ley lines, believes these geographical strongholds result from the "defilement of sin"—a condition brought on by such things as idolatrous worship, immorality, untimely bloodshed and broken covenants. He contends that unless and until these defiled areas are dealt with through repentance and renunciation they serve as "feeding troughs" for demons and their followers.[34]

Although ley lines are not the central focus of spiritual mapping, their presence, or perceived presence, in a community can suggest an important point of contact with the spirit world. For this reason, they should not be ignored.

Bear in mind, however, that research in this arena is risky. Many researchers waste valuable time documenting unimportant or nonexistent sites. Others invent leys or power centers, often to meet an assumed obligation, and wind up in serious deception. The only sure protection is to value substance over speculation and to insist that others test your conclusions.

COMMITMENT AND REVELATION

The best mappers are people who have made a conscious commitment to the land and community. Why? Because God reveals His secrets, and commands His blessing, to those who are serious enough to make relational and territorial covenants (see Deut. 11:10-15; Prov. 12:11,12; 27:18).

When Nehemiah heard that Jerusalem was in ruins, he wept, fasted, prayed and repented for several days (see Neh. 1:4-6). Soon afterwards he received the blessing of king Artaxerxes to rebuild the walls (see 2:6), and was granted divine success in all his undertakings—including research (see 2:11-15), recruiting (see 2:16-18), protective measures (see 4:8,9,15; 6:9-16), and governance (see 5:7-17; 13:7-31).

Commitment and blessing is a refrain that many of us have long since come to believe—at least intellectually. We can appreciate that God would share His secrets with His own, with those He knows He can trust. The hard part is the territorial aspect. The seemingly limiting notion that we are to embrace a *particular place*, to adopt its name and allow its blood to flow through our veins.

This act, however, is not as confining as it seems. As Scott Russell Sanders put it:

> To become intimate with your home region, to know the territory as well as you can, to understand your life as woven into the local life does not prevent you from recognizing and honoring the diversity of other places, cultures, ways. On the contrary, how can you value other places if you do not have one of your own? If you are not yourself *placed,* then you wander the world like a sightseer, a collector of sensations, with no gauge for measuring what you see.[35]

Even in captivity God spoke to His people about putting down roots, about making a long-term commitment to where they were. In Jeremiah 29:5-7 the Almighty admonished Jews living in Babylon:

> Build ye houses, and dwell in them; and plant gardens, and eat the fruit of them; take ye wives, and beget sons and daughters; and take wives for your sons, and give your daughters to husbands, that they may bear sons and daughters; that ye may be increased there, and not diminished. And seek the peace of the city whither I have caused you to be carried away captives, and pray unto the Lord for it: for in the peace thereof shall ye have peace (*KJV*).

Unfortunately, Sanders laments, "My nation's history does not encourage me, or anyone, to belong somewhere with a full heart. A vagabond wind has been blowing here for a long while, and it grows stronger by the hour."[36] While Sanders is an American, the same could be said of nations and peoples throughout the world. City dwellers are heading for the suburbs, while rural folk want to go to the city. People of the east want to experience the west, while southerners insist on moving north. The whole world has become a crossroads, a giant terminal where people nod silently to one another as they pass in opposite directions.

Success today is measured not by rootedness, but by motion—a term that is often mistaken for momentum. Clergy, far from being an exception to this rule, are a prime example. In the words of pastor Bob Beckett, they live and minister "with their emotional and spiritual bags packed."[37] They have the mentality of renters, not homeowners.

The differences are obvious. While an owner will generally treat his home with greater care, make improvements and get to know the neighbors, a short-term renter will seldom make these commitments. Because they have invested less, they have less to lose.

Sanders calls these two types of people inhabitants and migrants. He worries that the latter tend to "root themselves in ideas rather than places, in memories as much as in material things."[38] Lacking a territorial commitment they are less likely to know and care for the place they live in.

Ironically, migrants can sometimes be quite taken with spiritual mapping. What appeals to them, however, is the quest for knowledge, not changed communities. They enjoy the discovery of new truths but show little interest in applying them. Some become circuit-riding spiritual mappers, moving their research from town to town, often without being asked. But since their commitment is shallow, so are their conclusions.

Beckett is convinced that making a commitment to a community makes a vital difference in the unseen realm. This conviction stems partly from his own experience in Hemet and partly from the mail he receives from other church leaders. The primary theme of these letters is familiar—commitment and blessing. "Once they settled this commitment in their hearts," Beckett writes knowingly, "they seemed to receive new eyes with which to see both the evil and the redemptive elements in their cities."[39]

The commitment being defined here is an active engagement, not a passive lingering. "If you stay with a husband or wife out of laziness rather than love," Sanders asserts, "that is inertia, not marriage."[40] At the same time "there are voices enough, both inner and outer, urging us to deal with difficulties by pulling up stakes and heading for a new territory."[41] What we do with these voices offers a true gauge of our commitment.

Bob Beckett's method of silencing the voices urging him to leave Hemet was to purchase a grave plot on the edge of town. I visited it with him one day in late June 1998. Sadly, it was already occupied by the remains of a grandson who had died shortly after birth. His son-in-law, who had passed on a year later, was buried 50 yards away. As he wept silently over the headstones, it was obvious that they had become an integral part of the root system that anchored Bob to the community.

In his chapter on "House and Home," Scott Russell Sanders refers to a grisly headline that appeared in his local newspaper. It read: HOMELESS WOMAN CRUSHED WITH TRASH.

No one knows the woman's name, only that she crawled into a dumpster to sleep, was loaded into a truck, was compressed with the trash, and arrived dead at the incinerator. She wore white tennis shoes, gray sweatpants, a red windbreaker, and, on her left hand, 'a silver Indian Thunderbird ring.' Nearby residents had seen her climb into the dumpster, and later they heard the truck begin to grind, but they did not warn the driver soon enough, and so the woman died. Being homeless meant that she had already been discarded by family, neighbors, and community, and now she was gathered with the trash.[42]

"The more deeply I feel my own connection to home,"

Sanders concludes, "the more acutely I feel the hurt of those who belong to no place and no one."[43] He might well have been talking about the familiarity and fervor bred of spiritual mapping.

If familiarity and fervor are the offspring of commitment, however, they are also born of facts. Having already discussed what these facts are, we must now turn our attention to the business of finding them.

NOTES

1. Scott Russell Sanders, *Staying Put: Making a Home in a Restless World* (Boston, MA: Beacon Press, 1994), pp. xiii & 137.

2. Quoted in John Noble Wilford, *The Mapmakers* (New York: Vintage Books, 1981), p. 13.

3. It is possible, of course, to carry this feature to an extreme. As author Ptolemy Tompkins has noted: "Much of the area of the mind we have come to call the subconscious was, for the spiritual mapmakers of ancient America, subterranean. By allowing the hallucinatory landscape of dream a status alongside that of the physical world itself, these people created for themselves from the known world of rocks, rivers, and sky, a precarious dwelling place set about with openings into the world of disincarnate spirits" (*This Tree Grows Out of Hell* [San Francisco: HarperSanFrancisco, 1990], p. 16).

   Spiritual mappers can, if they are not careful, find themselves doing much the same thing. The danger in blending the subjective realm of imagination with the external world is that we are left with a view of reality that is either distorted or private. The first is dangerous while the latter is of limited value to others. To avoid superstition and/or irrelevance it is important to concentrate on your mission objectives and remain tethered to the Word of God.

4. Sanders, *Staying Put: Making a Home in a Restless World*, pp. 62, 63.

5. Ibid., p. 63.

6. H. W. F. Saggs, *The Greatness That Was Babylon* (London: Sidgwick & Jackson, 1962), pp. 315, 316.

7. T. K. Whipple, *Study Out The Land*. Quoted in *Reader's Digest*, "Points to Ponder" (September 1994), p. 162.

8. An example of the linkage between past and present is seen in the historic dialogue between Mansa Musa, the Emperor of Mali (A.D. 1312-1332), and the King of Yatenga. When the latter was asked to become a convert to Islam, he answered that he would first have to consult his ancestors by offering up sacrifices. See J. Ki-Zerbo, ed., *A General History of Africa:*

Methodology and African Prehistory (Berkeley: University of California Press & UNESCO, 1990), p. 16.

9. Edward Albert Shils, *Tradition* (Chicago: University of Chicago Press, 1981), p. 38.

10. Gary Snyder, *The Old Ways* (San Francisco: City Lights, 1977), p. 79.

11. Sanders, *Staying Put: Making a Home in a Restless World*, p. 111.

12. Ki-Zerbo, *A General History of Africa: Methodology and African Prehistory*, p. 17.

13. If domestic violence statistics are available on your community, they will likely be linked to districts or neighborhoods rather than individual addresses. This would be to protect the privacy of both victims and perpetrators.

14. The size of your paper will also depend upon the period of time you wish to chart.

15. Howard Rheingold, *The Virtual Community: Homesteading on the Electronic Frontier* (Reading, Mass.: Addison-Wesley, 1993), p. 1.

16. Ibid., p. 3. Rheingold reports that "the most addicted players of Minitel in France or Multi-User-Dungeons (MUDs) on the international networks, spend eighty hours a week or more pretending to be someone else, living a life that does not exist outside a computer" (p. 4).

17. Ley lines are thought to derive from, or be responsible for, the alignment of certain sacred sites. Researcher John Mitchell (from Cornwall, England) has identified 22 alignments between 53 megalithic sites over distances up to seven miles. See Rosemary Ellen Guiley, *Harper's Encyclopedia of Mystical & Paranormal Experience* (New York: Castle Books, 1991), pp. 329, 330.

18. Paul Devereux, *Earth Memory* (St. Paul: Llewellyn Publications, 1992), pp. 288, 289. According to British researcher Paul Devereux, "earth lights" have been seen, and studied, on every continent. During the 1905 Welsh Methodist Revival, for example, people living around Barmouth and Harlech saw light forms of all shapes and sizes dart across the ground and cling to rooftops—an occurrence that raises the question as to whether it was a sinister distraction or a demonic exodus. In the 1980s, Norwegians living in the valley of Hessdalen took hundreds of photographs of strange lights over a period of several years. So did English policemen conducting routine night patrols on moors around Skipton and Grassington. Additional sightings have been recorded around Scotland's Loch Leven, and Loughs Erne and Beg in Northern Ireland.

Traditional societies have long been aware of these lights and incorporated them into their world view. Early Chinese Buddhists, for example, determined that drifting globes of light observed from Wu-t'ai Shan were none other than the Bodhisattva of Wisdom, Manjushri (Edwin Bernbaum, *Sacred Mountains of the World* [San Francisco: Sierra Club Books, 1990], pp. 37, 39). The Yakima Indians of Washington State traditionally linked the flickering lights to divination rites, while the neighboring

Snohomish tribe considered them to be "doorways" into the Otherworld.

Others have maintained a less-inviting perspective on the subject. Michael Psellus, an eleventh century Byzantine writer, insisted the phenomena was evidence of demonic spirits called *lucifugi*, or "fly-the-lights." The Wintun tribe of Northern California saw the lights as malevolent "spirit eaters" and warned it was dangerous to get near them. In similar fashion, tribes living in the Himalayan foothills of northwest India believe the lights to be lantern-carrying men who, if approached, will spread illness or death. Malaysian natives see them as the spectral heads of women who have died in childbirth, while the African Ewe people contend they are produced by the magic of ju-ju men. To other tribes they are simply *aku*, or "the devil" (Devereux, *Earth Memory*, pp. 283-294).

In America, where the phenomena is colloquially referred to as "ghost" or "spook" lights, researchers have charted over one hundred sighting locations. Of these, the most prolific is the Chinati Mountains area near Marfa, Texas. Lights have been reported here for over a century. Early Apaches thought they were spirits. Although there is now an official viewing point on Highway 90, in the 1970s, two irreverent geologists actually chased the basketball-sized lights—unsuccessfully—in an off-road jeep.

"We know that lights can be produced during earthquake activity and powerful electrical storms," Devereux concedes, "but similar lights are also seen without either of these conditions being present." Devereux goes on to add that the lights usually measure one to two feet across, and definitely have a geography. "They usually haunt specific locales, either intensively for weeks, months, or even years, or else sporadically over decades or centuries" (Paul Devereux, *Places of Power* [London: Blandford, 1990], p. 66).

Sacred sites, including temples, hills and mountains, are typical hosts for earth lights phenomena. Glowing orbs have been seen cavorting over the Nazca Lines, the Great Pyramid at Giza, and around temples in Luxor and Darjeeling. American psychologist Alberto Villoldo and several companions reported seeing "an eerie light like a person" at Machu Picchu, while others have encountered strange lights and fleeting apparitions on the slopes of Northern California's Mount Shasta and on Pendle Hill in Lancashire, England. The latter, interestingly enough, was the gathering place of the seventeenth-century Pendle Witches, and the spot where the founder of the Quaker movement, George Fox, received his spiritual vision. Despite mounting evidence that earth lights exist, the question of what they *are* remains largely unanswered. Devereux prefers to look for geological and electromagnetic explanations for the earth lights phenomena, yet he admits that "the exact mechanism of their manifestation is not yet understood, and the energy involved is exotic...It seems to flicker in and out, as it were, on the very edge of physical manifestation" (Devereux, *Places of Power*, pp. 67, 68).

In an effort to get to the bottom of this mystery, Devereux, in early November 1977, assembled a team of twenty researchers—disciplines ranged from physics and chemistry to electronics and archaeology—to study unusual energy effects at ancient sacred sites throughout Great Britain. Tests included fault mapping, ultrasound and magnetic measurements, Kirlian electrophotography, radio propagation and infrared photography.

After taking several thousand readings at more than thirty locations, the team concluded that there were definite energy circuits within and around these sites. Evidentiary links included cyclical patterns of anomalous radio emissions, Geiger flares, and strong beta-radiation signatures (Devereux, *Places of Power*, pp. 49-54; see also James Swan, *The Power of Place* [Wheaton, Ill.: Quest Books, 1991], pp. 252, 253).

19. Guiley, *Harper's Encyclopedia of Mystical & Paranormal Experience*, pp. 329, 330.

20. Masons not only participated on the survey team that laid out America's federal district (including the ceremonial positioning of the initial cornerstone at Jones Point on the Potomac River), but they also dedicated the foundation stones of the United States Capitol and the White House with corn, wine and oil. See S. Brent Morris, *Cornerstones of Freedom: A Masonic Tradition* (Washington, D.C.: The Supreme Council, 33°, S. J., 1993), pp. 27-29.

21. See Nigel Pennick, *The Ancient Art of Geomancy* (Sebastopol, CA: CRCS Publications, 1979), p. 108; Albert Mackey, *An Encyclopedia of Freemasonry, Volume I* (New York: The Masonic History Company, 1915), p. 84.

22. The related field of peregrinology blends pilgrimage studies with sacred geography. See Rana Singh, "The Pilgrimage Mandala of Varanasi," in *Trends in the Geography of Pilgrimages*, (Varanasi, India: National Geographic Society of India, 1987), p. 170.

23. Patrick Tierney, *The Highest Altar* (New York: Viking Books, 1989), pp. 182, 184.

24. Ibid., pp. 154, 222.

25. Cerro Blanco, the major mountain deity at Nazca, is "married" to three other peaks—one at the coast, one in a range that gives life to the Nazca rivers, and one snowy crest 87 miles distant.

    From the Sun Temple at the center of the ancient Incan capital of Cuzco, Peru, 41 lines called *ceques* spread out into the country. Many of these invisible lines of force link up with coastal ritual sites and shrines atop sacred volcanoes.

26. The Qollahuayas are Bolivian diviners who once served as religious specialists for Inca royalty. They claim their power comes from ancestral graves on nearby Mount Kaata. See Joseph Bastien, *Mountain of the Condor* (Prospect Heights, Ill.: Waveland Press, 1978), p. 23.

27. Ibid., pp. 37-50.

28. Richard Anderson, "Geomancy," in Swan, *The Power of Place*, p. 197.

29. Medicine Grizzlybear Lake, "Power Centers" in Swan, *The Power of Place*, pp. 55, 57. Lake hastens to add that "Some of the power centers are negative sources of power, being the residences of bad spirits, forces, and energies."

30. Ibid., p. 52.

31. Ibid., p. 53.

32. George Otis, Jr., *The Twilight Labyrinth* (Grand Rapids: Chosen, 1997), p. 168.

33. Ibid., p. 192.

34. Alistair Petrie maintains that defiled people are attracted to defiled areas because like has a tendency to attract like. Over the years their own idolatrous activity reinforces the effect of the earlier defilement. Before the Israelites entered the Promised Land, demonic powers had already established a presence in the region. It was for this reason, Petrie believes, that God told the Hebrew children to "Destroy completely all the places on the high mountains and on the hills and under every spreading tree where the nations you are dispossessing worship their gods. Break down their altars, smash their sacred stones and burn their Asherah poles in the fire; cut down the idols of their gods and wipe out their names from those places" (Deut. 12:2,3).

35. Sanders, *Staying Put: Making a Home in a Restless World*, p. 114.

36. Ibid., p. xv.

37. Bob Beckett, *Commitment to Conquer* (Grand Rapids: Chosen, 1997), p. 71, (related items, pp. 64, 65).

38. Ibid., pp. 104, 106, 107.

39. Ibid., p. 69.

40. Sanders, *Staying Put: Making a Home in a Restless World*, p. 120.

41. Ibid., p. 102.

42. Ibid., p. 31.

43. Ibid., p. 32.

~❧~

GETTING THE FACTS

We have come to that stage of the spiritual mapping process that is undoubtedly the most time consuming, and perhaps the most complex. Whether you call it data acquisition, spiritual discovery or simply the investigation, it is the shoe-leather dimension of any research project.

Until now, we have concentrated largely on spiritual mapping preparation. We have discussed the importance of making a commitment to the community, determining the parameters of an investigation and assembling a quality research team. We have also explored, at least in general terms, the kind of information we want, and various ways of looking at it.

This chapter, however, will offer practical advice on actually doing research— and doing it *correctly*. After all, the ultimate purpose for launching a spiritual mapping campaign is to acquire valuable insights that will lead to the transformation of a community. The following collection of tips will make locating and organizing pertinent information more rewarding for veterans and beginners alike.

Community familiarization is arguably the most important homework assignment any intercessor can take on. While amateurs can indeed participate in this process, they should be individuals who aspire to a higher standard of excellence. Those who tackle spiritual intelligence gathering should be committed to doing whatever it takes to succeed.

That being said, it's time to hit the books—and the streets!

FINDING THE BEST SOURCES

There are essentially four ways in which a spiritual mapper can gather useful research data:

1. Observe human environments and behavior
2. Conduct interviews
3. Examine print and media materials
4. Listen to God in prayer

Any one of these methods can supply a veritable trea-suretrove of interesting and relevant data, but good researchers will seek to combine all four. In a moment we'll take a closer look at each of these methods.

Before we move on, however, it is important to pause long enough to examine the distinction between *primary* and *secondary* sources. In brief, primary sources—which can include anything from artifacts to census reports to people—offer direct information, whereas secondary sources—which may include books, articles and dissertations—are generally interpretive in nature.

Which is more useful? The answer is that relevant information comes from relevant sources. It does not matter whether these sources are books, institutions or people. What is important is that they deliver information that is both accurate and germane to the issues you are investigating. Articles and conversations that are merely interesting won't get the job done. If you want to maximize your time on the research trail, try to stick with guides that will keep you pointed in the right direction.

WHERE INFORMATION HIDES

Investigation is an important part of the spiritual mapping process. This is because crucial information is often hidden. Sometimes critical data rests like the proverbial needle in a haystack. At other times, it is disguised, like a chameleon, in plain sight. On only the rarest occasions will it come up and bite you on the nose.

As you consider how the enemy has deployed his assets in your community, it is wise to keep two things in mind. First, he almost never places all of his eggs in one basket. Obvious strongholds, such as idolatrous temples or sex clubs, are only a part of his strategy. It is appropriate to note the nature and extent of these traps, but you will also need to document any number of less conspicuous (but equally deadly) snares.

The second thing to remember is that the enemy's primary field of assault is the human mind. His constant ambition is to elevate himself and to destroy that which is precious to God. He accomplishes this by introducing deceptive memes (powerful, self-replicating ideas) and by facilitating the development of neural memory patterns that are conducive to his purposes.[1] Once these psychic platforms are in place he can (and does) use them to control human communities.

Gaining entrance to these "head nests" is not always easy. Some people never open the door, while others do so only with reluctance. Unfortunately, there is no better, or more important, place to observe the enemy's handiwork. As a competent spiritual mapper you need to get into these hidden workshops. And the best way to do this is through interviews.

WHO WOULD KNOW?

The search for quality information sources may force you to play detective. Key questions to ask yourself are, *Who would know? Who would care? Who would care enough to put it in print?* It is amazing how resourceful the mind can be when asked the right questions.

If you are looking for accurate community crime statistics, for example, you will probably want to contact local law enforcement (the police and district attorney), home and corporate security firms, victim support agencies and insurance companies. All of these sources will have a direct interest in the kind of statistics you are searching for. Even if they do not produce or distribute relevant data themselves, they will certainly be able to point you in the right direction.

Selecting sound human sources is a bit more complicated. Great care should be taken in choosing interview subjects.

Beginners often make the mistake of rushing after the first name that occurs to them. However, there is no guarantee that people who are well known, active in the community or go to church will yield a useful interview.

So what kind of individuals do qualify as useful respondents? To begin with, it is critical that your candidate understands thoroughly the vocabulary, history and rituals of the cultural environment you wish to study. If they do not, you will likely elicit little more than surmises and pseudo-analysis. It is also important to ascertain whether the respondent is currently involved in the culture. If they have dropped out in recent years (for example, an American Indian who has moved off the reservation into a suburban Anglo neighborhood), they will be limited in their ability to provide you with up-to-date information.

With these caveats in mind, your search for worthy respondents should gravitate toward people with good memories, unique roles, performance skills and long lives. Folklife scholars often refer to such individuals as "tradition bearers." If you don't know anyone fitting this description, the best places to start looking are in local churches, community centers and stores, small parks where people gather, historical societies and ethnic and community festivals. Once you find a tradition bearer, the pace of your investigation will likely quicken. This is due to their unique ability to untangle historical chronologies and then relate these events to contemporary attitudes and practices.

Good interview sources can also include press and media personnel, social workers, religious leaders and practitioners, government officials, artists and performers, educators and researchers, law enforcement officials, students and retirees. In evaluating each individual candidate, you will want to consider both their knowledge base and their ability to give adequate time to your project.

Harder to find, but exceedingly valuable when you do, are respondents associated with false religions, illicit practices and alternative lifestyles. Examples of such people might include high degree Freemasons, teenage Goths, Buddhist lamas, religious lesbians or practicing witches. While your Christian upbringing may have steered you away from these people and the cultures they inhabit, this does not make them insignificant or illusory. To the contrary, many of these groups have grown dramatically in recent years—and not just in the West.

So how do you determine if these or similar groups are active in your community? And if they are, where do you go to find out more about them? Who do you talk to?

The truth is that most cities today have vast underground networks that encompass everything from gang turf, gay bars, pagan covens and voodoo circles. To access these subcultures you will need to identify entry points—like spiritual metro stations—that can take you beneath the streets. Depending on the network, these may be temple or church visitor centers, art houses, campus affinity clubs or metaphysical bookstores. Although these locations are attached to a specific ideology or practice, outsiders are welcomed—either as customers or as potential converts. Display genuine interest or curiosity and you may well be invited to attend a non-advertised meeting. If and when this happens, you will have your ticket to the spiritual underground.

WAITING ON GOD FOR RESEARCH LEADS

Finding good sources also involves waiting upon God. Nobody knows better than He where community secrets are kept. If you have attempted to do the Lord's bidding in the past, you probably know what it means to be nudged by the Holy Spirit. As John's Gospel reminds us, the Master's voice has a familiar tone. It stands as a reliable source of revelation, counsel and correction.

This is not to say there is no warning label on divine guidance. In fact, every spiritual mapping team must be careful not to mistake *research leads* for *research conclusions*. God is not doing our work for us—He is graciously pointing us in the right direction.

The appropriate response is to thank Him for the tip and then roll up our sleeves. Divine appointments are great, but we must still conduct the interview.

❦

NOBODY KNOWS BETTER THAN GOD WHERE COMMUNITY SECRETS ARE KEPT.

❦

Insights gleaned in the place of prayer also need to be verified and supplemented with objective evidence. It is this evidence, not the subjective impressions that lead to it, that will ultimately give your report credibility.

OBSERVATION STRATEGY AND TECHNIQUE

In the trench warfare of World War I, the area between the respective lines was known as no-man's-land. Not surprisingly, patrol duty in this dangerous strip was very unpopular and casualties were common. At the same time, however, the side that was willing to patrol aggressively in no-man's-land gained substantial intelligence and tactical advantages. The side that hesitated to enter this difficult area was handicapped.

This is true with spiritual mapping. If you want to obtain a good look at the enemy's deployments and deceptive weaponry in your community, you must be prepared to reconnoiter the front lines. While this will not always prove enjoyable, it will provide you with insights unobtainable from the pew.

The focus of your observational patrols should be on *places* where enemy activity has assumed distinctive proportions and on human *behaviors* that offer evidence of demonic allegiances or a renewed hunger for godly values.

GRID MAPPING

This activity involves the systematic notation of *spiritual quest sites* (temples, shrines, burial grounds, New Age bookstores) and *social bondage sites* (brothels, porno theaters, gay bars, crackhouses) inside the research area.[2] Each sector of the community should be canvassed thoroughly. Mobile unit workers should concentrate on one city block at a time. (Rural areas can be subdivided more liberally since they generally contain fewer relevant survey sites.) Each entry should include a detailed description of the site and a complete address—the latter lending itself to an eventual data set.

It is important not to rush this process. Many mappers register only those sites that seem obvious and neglect to investigate addresses that have no discernible relevance. This risks overlooking some of the most significant worship and social bondage sites in the community. For instance, a Christian woman visiting a furniture store in New Orleans reported seeing a back warehouse containing ritual candles and the bones of scores of sacrificial animals. On another occasion, a pastor's wife in Washington state arrived early to an appointment at a naturopathic clinic to find the proprietress seated on the floor in a circle of candles and incense. Illicit business, it should be noted, is almost always transacted behind closed doors.

While unmarked sites can be difficult to detect, there are ways to improve your odds. Besides asking for the leading of the Holy Spirit, you can casually interrogate neighborhood "old-timers," as well as the residents and shopkeepers adjacent to unmarked buildings (don't overlook second-story addresses). You can also ask your archival unit colleagues to dig up any public records that might shed light on the function and ownership of a given establishment.

Although shopping malls, sporting arenas and even restaurants can also facilitate serious bondage, these sites would not generally be tallied since they are equally capable of serving legitimate purposes. Of course, if you should find a glaring exception to this, be sure to note it.

Poverty-ridden neighborhoods should also be treated carefully. Although they are prime social bondage scenes, there is a moral distinction between poverty and vice. Godly people can be poor, but they cannot be unrighteous.

Attempts to identify significant features (such as ley lines) within the layout of the community are premature during this micro-mapping phase. While this activity has become quite popular—even dominant—in some spiritual mapping circles, it is easily distracting and often misleading. Even if Freemasons or other geomantic planners can be shown to have been involved with the original city layout, this is but a single piece of a much larger puzzle. Keep it in perspective.

ACTIVITY AND EVENT RECORDING

Your second observational assignment involves recording noteworthy patterns of behavior—especially community events. These might include religious ceremonies and pilgrimages, policy-making processes (city council and board of education meetings), social protest or advocacy events (anti-abortion picketing, gay pride parades), and various Christian gatherings.

In observing these and other activities you should consider, at a minimum, the following five elements:

1. Form: *What is being done and in what way?*
2. Duration: *How long does it last?*
3. Frequency: *How often does it occur?*
4. Antecedent: *What happened before?*
5. Consequent patterns: *What follows?*

There will be occasions when the activity you are observing becomes exceptionally busy or intense. Your senses will flood with new images, and your mind will try desperately to sort them into meaningful categories or patterns. When this happens, you may need to temporarily retreat from the subject or activity. This will give your overwhelmed mind time to catch up with its processing. By pausing to download backlogged images you will be able to view the next scene refreshed.

Remember, too, that human beings are extremely complex subjects. If you are going to observe their behavior, you will need to suppress hasty conclusions. Inferential leaps can, and invariably will, land you in very hot water. (I will have more to say about drawing safe conclusions in chapter 9.)

Observing people is an activity that requires considerable skill and tact. Even if your subject has given you permission to watch them, they are likely to alter their behavior out of self-consciousness. If they have not acceded to being observed, they may respond with hostility or withdraw altogether. Knowing when to pull back and when to press in is critical to your success.

As a general rule of thumb you can safely observe public figures (politicians, artists, educators) or figures in public (demonstrators, shoppers, travelers). Private persons in private settings should not be observed except by permission. Violating this rule is not just bad manners; in some cases it may be illegal. Spiritual fact-finding has nothing to do with voyeurism and stalking.

Public activities and events, though generally appropriate for observation, can occasionally be tricky. While artistic performances, street marches and political debates are clearly intended for public consumption, things like sexual activity, drug and alcohol consumption and religious rituals fall into a gray area. Some actions, even though they are performed in public, have private connotations. The wisest approach is to familiarize yourself with local etiquette and protocols and then ask individuals you wish to observe if they mind you doing so. Some may consent to being watched, but object to be photographed or recorded. Take what you can get.

In most social settings, it is extremely difficult to observe without being observed. It is better to let people know why you are among them and then act human. Trying to cloak your activities or intentions will only arouse suspicion. If note taking proves awkward you have two options. The first is to speak your observations into a microcassette recorder that is placed in your breast pocket, purse or handbag. (The latter work best if you are seated at a table.) The other option is to make mental notes and then transfer them to a notepad or handheld computer. This can be done inconspicuously in lavatories, stairwells or phone cubicles. If these facilities do not exist, or you are blessed with an exceptional memory, you can also transfer your notes at home immediately following the event.

The Art of Interviewing

No aspect of spiritual mapping research is more important than interviewing. This, as I noted earlier, is because the most insidious and profound bondages reside in people's minds. As Christian liberators, we need to understand precisely what we are dealing with. This involves ascertaining both the extent of the enemy's campaign and the nature of his enchantments. It requires us to learn where his strongholds lie, and how many of our fellow citizens have already been taken captive.

The best way of doing this is to ask members of our community to take us on a tour of their inner worlds. Interviews, by drawing out vital confessions and descriptions, can serve as the vehicle for this journey. They can permit us to observe whatever might be lurking beyond the limits of our vision.

Some interviews, of course, will be more mundane. But even these, if handled with the right touch, can yield a dazzling assortment of useful details. People are essentially walking databases. Treat them with respect and they will help you confirm or dispute key facts, add nuances to your analyses, and secure useful leads for follow-up.

ARRANGING AND PREPARING FOR INTERVIEWS

Before you begin contacting potential respondents, it is a good idea to set up a master planner. This activity road map can be in hard copy or electronic form and should include a list of key questions, promising sources, pending and confirmed appointments, logistical details and follow-up actions. If you take the time to develop and update this planner, you will always know where your project stands.

Your next step will be to develop a statement of purpose that can introduce your project to potential interview subjects. This document should offer a satisfactory explanation to those who want to know who you represent and how the information you collect will be used. Although you don't need to elaborate everything, make an effort to use language that non-Christians will understand. You might, for example, explain that you are part of a multi-church research effort designed to better equate Christians with the community's early history and current needs. Moreover, you intend to use the information you gather to pray for the community's welfare and to pinpoint areas of potential service.

With your statement of purpose in hand, it is time to begin contacting potential respondents. Each of these people should be selected according to the criteria outlined in the "Who Would Know?" section at the beginning of this chapter.

When arranging interviews, be sure to display the utmost courtesy. This means, among other things, not unduly imposing on your subject's schedule. Allot plenty of lead time so that you can arrange a mutually convenient appointment. It is also good form to offer to meet your interviewee at a location that is of their choosing. If they select a restaurant, call the establishment in advance to prearrange for a quiet table and payment.

If your subject is a recent immigrant or an older member of a minority community, be sure to ascertain before the meeting whether or not they speak your language. This is an especially important step if your conversation will be processed by a third party (such as a secretary). If your subject does not speak well enough to be understood by you *and* a transcriber, you will need to arrange for an interpreter.

Background research is another important part of interview preparation. Learn as much as you can about your contact and their area of expertise before calling on them. They will respect you for having done your homework. After your preliminary research has yielded an initial set of interview questions, take a few minutes to review the list and edit out anything that seems repetitive or unnecessary. This exercise will help insure a lively and productive line of inquiry. You don't want to waste your respondent's time by asking questions that you could have answered yourself.

Finally, don't neglect to follow up each interview with a note or call thanking your subject for their time. Stanley Payne's *The Art of Asking Questions* offers an excellent rationale for this protocol:

> People are being exceedingly gracious when they consent to be interviewed. We may ask them to give us anywhere from a few minutes to hours of their time in a single interview. We may ask them to expose their ignorance with no promise of enlightenment. We may try to probe their innermost thinking on untold subjects. We may sometimes request their cooperation before telling them who the sponsor is and before indicating the nature of our questions—for fear of prejudicing their answers. All this, yet they submit to being interviewed. And without promise of even a penny for their thoughts![3]

BUILDING RAPPORT

Rapport between a researcher and his informant often builds over four stages:

1. Apprehension: *The subject will usually give short, crisp answers.*
2. Exploration: *The subject will internalize questions like: Who is*

this individual? Can they be trusted? What do they really want from these interviews?

3. Cooperation: *The subject spontaneously corrects the assumptions and pronunciations of the interviewer.*
4. Participation: *The informant becomes a full-blown teacher of the researcher.*

While participation, or at least cooperation, is what you want from your informant, this may not be achievable in a single conversation. A better idea, if you are planning or hoping for a series of interviews, is to devote the initial meeting to relationship building rather than the eliciting of information.

Remember that you are a visitor to your subject's world. They are likely to act as good hosts, but you must be a good guest. Among other things this means being perceived as a learner—or at least an enthusiastic listener. Listening in the highest sense of the word is taking on the role of the other. To be a good role taker you must "stand" with each respondent in the latter's relationship to the universe, and view it and its associated vocabulary from that perspective. The role-taking process is the first stage of understanding, and it requires systematic listening without applying one's own analytic categories.

As a researcher, you believe "everything" and "nothing" simultaneously. You may nod "yes" at every statement, but the nod is a sign of understanding, not necessarily of agreement.

TIPS FOR EFFECTIVE INTERVIEWING

Experience has shown that 60- to 90-minute interviews are the most productive. Stretch things out and you run the risk of fatiguing or annoying your subject. Still have ground to cover? Ask politely for a follow-up session. (If this is not possible, they may offer to extend the conversation.) In the end, the number of sessions you will need depends solely upon the knowledge and availability of your subject.

To get the most out of your interview you might want to take Robert Newton Peck's blunt advice: "Never miss a chance to keep your mouth shut."[4] Let your subject talk! The purpose of the interview, after all, is for them to enlighten you. Some degree of rambling is to be expected. Unless it goes on too long or gets too far afield, stay cool. It may take you in a valuable new direction. (It is also important to remember that some cultures, such as Arab and Native American, communicate more slowly. Be prepared to exercise patience when interviewing these subjects.)

With experience you will develop a set of tactical measures for steering "runaways" and loosening the tongue-tied. These measures include appropriate gestures and expressions, as well as a host of useful vocal prompts. For example:

To fish for more detail, you might say,
"Tell me more about that" or "That's very interesting."

In order to probe chronology you can ask,
"And then?" or "When was that?"

If you are seeking clarification, try remarking,
"I don't quite understand" or "But you said earlier..."

To elicit an explanation, offer a question,
"Why?" or "How come?"

While it is a good idea to keep a list of questions or topics handy during the interview, your material and sequencing should be flexible enough to maintain a natural conversational style. After all, what else are you going to do when the respondent, while answering your first question, also fully answers the third and some of question six?

When structuring a line of inquiry, try to balance brevity against clarity. You certainly don't want your interview littered with redundant or superficial questions. But neither can you afford to walk away from the discussion in a state of confusion. If it takes seven questions to fully explore a particular subject, don't hesitate to ask them.

DISCOVERY QUESTIONS ARE DESIGNED TO ELICIT HARD, CORE FACTS ABOUT THE SPIRITUAL CONDITION OF YOUR COMMUNITY.

It is also important that you not leave your subject confused. Have you provided them with the information necessary to answer your questions? Do you need to be more specific? Have you ventured into topics that are unrelated to their personal experience? Have you tripped them up with marathon and/or multi-part questions? If you take care in these matters, your respondent will take care of you.

In any interview the specific questions you ask will depend on the needs of your project and the capabilities of your subject. If you are just starting out and don't know what to ask, you may want to peruse the checklist of discovery questions located at the back of this book. This can help focus your thinking.

Discovery questions are designed to elicit hard, core facts about the spiritual condition of your community. They are fundamental to the spiritual mapping process and may not be neglected or exchanged. At the same time, good interviewers will often supplement these inquiries with what ethnologists have come to call *descriptive questions*. These questions (five examples of which are listed below) are designed to extract vivid and accurate details about people, places and procedures. Many interviews are not complete without them.

Grand Tour Question:

"Could you describe a typical visit to the temple?"

Mini-Tour Question:

"What happens during the purification ritual?"

Example Question:

"Could you give me an example of the types of incense used?"

Experience Question:

"What was it like when you made your first offering?"

Native Language Question:

"How would you refer to this ceremony?"

RECORDING THE CONVERSATION

It is not possible to write down everything that goes on, or gets said, during the course of an interview. At best, your notes represent a substantially condensed version of what actually occurred. And yet, because these clipped phrases, single words and unconnected sentences were recorded on the spot, they are of enormous value.

This said, there are several things you can do to improve the quality of your records. If you take your notes by hand, consider double-spacing them to preserve legibility. This can make a big difference whenever ideas are flowing rapidly, or you happen to encounter weather or terrain hazards (potholes are a notorious menace).

An even better way of recording important interviews is on microcassettes. This unobtrusive media allows you to retain nearly every word uttered during a discussion—a feature that virtually eliminates follow-up caused by incomplete notes. Today's microrecorders come in a wide range of styles and prices, and as with most products, you generally get what you pay for. Look for devices with good audio pick up, dual tape speeds, dating and cueing capability and a pause button. Most of these are now standard features. (Even when recording, it is always a good idea to take written notes as a backup.)

The one drawback associated with microcassettes, and it is a minor one, is that they require special transcription equipment. This, however, seems a small price to pay for something that will ultimately save considerable time and money. In the end you are purchasing an asset that can be used repeatedly.

Another problem to be overcome is the fact that many people are ill at ease around recording devices. To lessen this anxiety, simply explain that the tape will be used to help you remember all of their valuable comments. You might also say that you don't know shorthand and that experience has taught you not to trust your memory. Most people will accept these explanations. From here you can go on to spend the next few minutes in casual conversation. Start the recording device when the subject is no longer focused on it. Leave some space at the beginning of each tape so you can later fill in the date, location and persons present. This will serve as a backup in the event the tape label is somehow lost or destroyed.

One word of caution. Be sure to place the recorder close enough to the subject that it will pick up their comments. This is particularly important if the respondent has a soft voice or there is significant background noise. Restaurants, parks and automobiles offer notoriously poor recording environments. Your best bet is to avoid them. If this is proves impossible, try to find a quiet spot.

Voice-activated recorders offer certain advantages, but they have a nasty tendency to cut off the first word or two of each sentence. They can also make it difficult to suppress irrelevant remarks. Using a pause button will allow you to be more discriminating in terms of what you actually record.

After you have completed your interview, label your tape and get it transcribed as soon as possible. The final transcript should identify each speaker (initials are okay), and present a clean semantic flow (nominal corrections are permissible for the sake of readability). It should also include a "summary sheet" containing the name of the interviewer and respondent(s), the interview date and location, a listing of the main topics of discussion and, if possible, a short profile of the respondent.

USING SECONDARY RESOURCES

Secondary resources offer spiritual mappers yet another means of hunting elusive information. The quarry, in this case, can reside in anything from books and dissertations to newspapers and census data. It can even hide in personal records such as letters, diaries and journals, although these sources are often classified as "primary."

This is the domain of the archival unit. If you are a denizen of the local library, a connoisseur of endnotes or a veteran web surfer, welcome home. You have a lot of work ahead of you, and hopefully the following pages will make your task just a little bit easier.

An obvious starting point in the field of secondary research is publications. An enormous amount of useful information has been written down over the years, and it is your job to ferret out those pages that might be of value to your project. As you proceed with this task, it is always important to ask when a particular document was written, who wrote it and what was going on in the world or community at the time. Expect to find tremendous differences in style and usefulness. Some items will be well written and yet contain little of value. Others will be threadbare in style and yet sumptuous in content.

Instinct, of course, plays a significant role in source evaluation. But it is not your only measuring stick. There are any number of objective questions that may be asked. For example, does the title suggest a special perspective on the topic? If the source is a book, is the publishing company well known and respected? If the source is a periodical, does it specialize in certain subjects and is it well respected? What is the publication date? Does the source define the topic sufficiently? Does it acknowledge other views? Does it include clear footnotes and a bibliography? Is it interesting and easy to read?

If you are looking for source material on local history, your search may be impacted by your location. If you live in a region that has produced an important personality, you will find that more has been written about your area. The same thing goes for sites that abound in natural wonders or have been the scene of some national event. While the history of a lesser-known place is just as important, it may not be quite as easy to track down.

A library is always a good first stop for any researcher. In addition to learning what others have discovered about your topic, you will also find an assortment of guides (such as maps and directories) for conducting your own research. Having a clearly defined set of research objectives will help librarians know how best to direct you. Even when you don't find anything useful in a particular source (or place), take a moment to note the negative results as an aide-memoir.

If you are new to this kind of research, or could simply use a refresher on the merits of various resources, I invite you to review the sample profiles listed below. Although limited in both category and content, they should still provide you with a decent idea of what is out there—and how to go about finding it.

BOOKS

For serious research work, nothing beats a good book. To begin with, books are compact and portable, a handy feature if you need to take your source material on the road. They can also be marked with highlighters (to tag relevant passages) and reproduced in photocopiers (so these passages can be placed into appropriate files). Books can provide anything from stories and statistics to leads and analysis. Their comprehensive format, unlike periodicals, encourages in-depth investigation. Thousands of new titles are published every year, and it is a good bet that the local library or bookstore has something related to your subject.

DISSERTATIONS

If you are looking for a source that can provide detailed case studies and thoughtful analysis on a wide variety of themes, consider dissertations, the academic *coup de grâce* of doctoral students. What makes these so valuable is the fact that they are produced under rigorous guidelines and supervision—a requirement that often results in tightly reasoned arguments and a useful listing of related primary and secondary sources. Directories of student dissertations can be accessed at most colleges and universities, as well as the Library of Congress.

NEWSPAPERS

The city daily is not only the fastest printed vehicle for breaking news and commentary, but it is also a prime source of local history. In fact, in the days before television and radio, newspapers were the lifelines of public communication. Many libraries and city publishers maintain catalogued archives of past editions on microfilm or microfiche. These are definitely worth a visit. In addition to describing the facts associated with certain issues or events, newspaper articles can also provide the names of knowledgeable individuals you may want to track down and interview.

MAGAZINES AND JOURNALS

These popular resources, although a bit slower than newspapers and the electronic media when it comes to delivering breaking news, more than compensate for their pace by offering greater substance and accuracy. Many are also thematic, providing readers with a steady diet of related articles. (They are specialty stores rather than department stores.) The primary distinction between magazines and journals is that the latter tend to be more analytical and are often associated with professional institutions.

PUBLIC RECORDS
This huge and rarely accessed collection of sources includes census statistics, city council minutes, board of education proceedings, legislative bills and agendas, local and regional histories, anniversary booklets and property use records. While all of this information is in the public domain, few people outside of the legal and journalistic professions ever make use of it. You should. With a little initiative and payment of nominal fees, you can acquire copies of almost any recorded document.

WEBSITES
As many devoted web surfers have discovered, the Internet offers a veritable smorgasbord of interesting data collections. These can be found on large sites maintained by governments, academic institutions and news organizations, and on informal pages serviced by enterprising individuals. In most cases, posted information can be downloaded onto your home computer for further review.

BROADCAST DOCUMENTARIES
Nearly every day of the year some type of investigative report or documentary special is broadcast over network, cable and satellite television channels. Many of these deal with historical, social and religious themes that are of particular interest to spiritual mappers. With a bit of advance planning (requiring a TV guide and videocassette recorder), you can not only watch the broadcast but also make your own personal copy. Pay close attention because many of these documentaries will provide excellent leads for follow-up research.

PERSONAL RECORDS AND STUDIES
Diaries, letters, journals, family albums and genealogies are all useful tools for researching local history. They offer valuable comments on daily life and common concerns, especially as they relate to local affairs, economic problems and religious and social con-

troversies. The best way to locate private source material is to start with your own friends, neighbors and extended family members. You can also run a notice in area newspapers, work through the local historical society, nose around auctions and secondhand bookstores, or solicit leads from the town's "old-timers."

THE ROLE OF THE INTERCESSOR

Intercessors are perhaps the most poorly understood element of the spiritual mapping process. On some teams, they are elevated to the status of divine oracles, rendering the work of other units largely unimportant. More often, they are underutilized, relegated to a role of supporting the "real workers." Either way, the team, and the project, are hampered.

In actual fact, the intercessory unit has much to contribute to a spiritual mapping campaign. Its members can pray that their field colleagues will be granted divine appointments, that they will find favor with respondents, and that God will surround them with His protection. They can ask the Holy Spirit to lead archival researchers to hidden and/or confirming sources. They can petition for wisdom in the selection of project boundaries, the setting of schedules, and the evaluation of people and information. Finally, they can pray that God will prepare a ready audience for the final report.

Intercessors can also collect valuable information through the discipline of waiting on God. This information may come in the form of leads about people, places or issues, understanding of complex patterns or hidden meanings, or confirmation of certain facts or hypotheses. Whatever their shape or nature, these divine contributions are important enough to be written down in a systematic fashion. This is done not with the idea of creating an addendum to the Holy Scriptures, but rather as a means of remembering and recovering contextual revelation.

MAINTAINING PRAYER LOGS

Team intercessors are at liberty to personalize their prayer journals so long as key elements, such as writing style and layout, remain consistent and legible. This is important because the prayer log is ultimately a public document, a working record. As such, it requires a clean and disciplined layout that includes, but is not limited to, a logical dating system and standardized entries. Some intercessors may find they need to make adjustments in their normal routine in order to harmonize with other team members and the public requirements of the project.

Entries should be recorded immediately at the conclusion of each prayer session. This will help protect against memory fade and insure that divine revelation is considered in a timely fashion. Each record or comment should be as concise as possible to avoid confusion. Subjective impressions and conjecture may be included but only if it is labeled for what it is.

The next thing I would urge team intercessors to consider is a coding system for tagging certain types of recurring entries. Four obvious examples are prayer themes, subjective impressions, answered prayer, and specific action items. There should also be a way to index related entries spread out over different days and pages. This can be done manually with margin codes, or automatically with certain computer programs (assuming the journal is maintained electronically). Finally, the journal should have a system for cross-referencing subject entries, so analysts can look at the contents from various perspectives.

So what can a researcher learn from a prayer log? If it has been well maintained by a godly and experienced intercessor, just about anything. In the end, there is nothing more exhilarating than the knowledge that God has spoken to us, and that His words have provided the keys to unlock deceptive strongholds in our community.

TEAMWORK IN DATA GATHERING

Individual researchers are faced with significant limitations. They cannot be in two places at the same time; they can work only a limited number of hours before wearing down; and they suffer from the lack of an objective second set of eyes. The logical remedy for these deficiencies is, of course, teamwork.

Not surprisingly, there are numerous references in Scripture to the advantages of collaboration (see Exod. 17:12; Judg. 20:11; Neh. 4; Luke 10:1). The writer of Ecclesiastes declares:

> Two are better than one, because they have a good return for their work: If one falls down, his friend can help him up. But pity the man who falls and has no one to help him up! Also, if two lie down together, they will keep warm. But how can one keep warm alone? Though one may be overpowered, two can defend themselves. A cord of three strands is not quickly broken (4:9-12).

The key to successful teamwork is getting a collection of individuals to operate harmoniously—something that means more than just getting along with one's colleagues. It is also a matter of integrating special talents and assignments in such a way that the full potential of the group is exploited. In order to accomplish this a team must have a clearly defined mission, a competent team leader and well-trained personnel with complimentary assignments.

One of the advantages of a team operation is the ability to employ collective memory. By assigning individual team members different categories of information to observe and remember, the volume of new data to be retained is reduced to manageable increments.

The only time collective observation doesn't work well is during interviews or in sensitive research environments. In these situations, a large group can be intrusive and conspicuous. To avoid causing a scene or inciting potential conflict, keep your operating units small—no more than two to four people.

Partnering assignments should be based on factors like gender, experience, personality and linguistic proficiency. Mission awareness is also important, as is each member's willingness to subordinate personal interests for the common good. If you are a team leader, get to know your personnel. Be prepared to reassign them to take advantage of new and changing circumstances. This might involve a situation that requires a single gender unit. On another day, you might need a special combination of talent, such as computer experts, interviewers or linguists. Other circumstances may call for a more experienced or mature unit.

Team members should also be prepared to take on certain practical responsibilities. This means that in addition to their data acquisition assignments they will need to record daily reports, handle budgetary matters, give computer tutorials or lead team devotions. It is up to the team leader to insure that a mechanism is in place (planning meetings or memos) that will keep members updated on the overall progress of the campaign.

ORGANIZING YOUR DATA

"Organizing," as Winnie the Pooh creator A. A. Milne once said, "is what you do before you do something, so that when you do it, it's not all mixed up."[5] This is of particular import in spiritual mapping work. The substantial body of information that is generated demands sound organizational plans and skills. In just the first few weeks of your campaign, you are likely to amass a broad assortment of items ranging from maps and source lists to articles and interview transcripts. If these materials are not carefully organized from the outset, your team can easily find itself paralyzed (not to mention frustrated) when it comes time to draw conclusions.

To help you to avoid the pitfalls that come from sloppy organizing, the following sections will suggest practical ways to organize various data records such as microcassettes and field notes. These will instruct you how to prepare your gleanings for subsequent analysis. After all, it is not how much information you collect but what you do with it that counts.

INFORMATION CONTROL SYSTEMS

Proper management of project materials involves a good deal of time, attention and patience. Your files and tapes must be carefully labeled and logged, transcripts must be filed logically, and books must be put in their proper place on the shelf. However mundane these tasks may seem, they will pay off in the end by rendering your materials accessible and useful.

It is a good idea to set up at least two files—one for project administration and one for project research. Administrative file headings might include "Plans and Outlines," "Schedules and Appointments," and "Budget Items." The research file should be subdivided according to the categories outlined in chapter 6. Active folders should contain items such as maps, tape logs, interview transcripts, field notes, relevant articles, government statistics or photocopied book material.

The important thing is to organize your notes according to their *intended use* rather than their source. Do, however, record the source of every note because you may want to return to it to check for accuracy or pick up additional information. Set a regular time, perhaps once a month, to review, condense and organize your files. Dispose of any excess chaff to avoid clutter and confusion.

THE DATA SEGREGATION DEBATE

Some spiritual mapping projects have elected to maintain a wall of separation between their archival, mobile and intercessory units. The intent of this barrier has been to build an extra set of checks and balances into the spiritual mapping process. While this approach has, in at least one instance, produced impressive results, other campaigns will need to weigh these potential benefits against those of a unified operation.

~≋~

SUCCESSFUL SPIRITUAL MAPPING ALSO REQUIRES THAT TEAMS DISCERN THE MEANING OF THE FACTS THEY COLLECT. INFORMATION WITHOUT UNDERSTANDING IS LIKE A CAR WITHOUT FUEL.

~≋~

The rewards of a collaborative program are significant. In addition to the clear benefits of shared leads and cooperative assessment, there are also advantages to maintaining one set of data files. It is not only expensive to keep up multiple file systems; but if the team is not in routine communication, there is a good chance that certain information sources will be harvested twice.

Data acquisition, while exhilarating and rewarding in itself, is only half the equation. Successful spiritual mapping also requires that teams discern the meaning of the facts they collect. Information without understanding is like a car without fuel. It can be collected and admired, but it will not be able to take you anywhere. To help you avoid this predicament, our next chapter will explore the all-important process of drawing conclusions from raw data.

NOTES

1. For a detailed explanation of these concepts see George Otis, Jr., *The Twilight Labyrinth*, (Grand Rapids: Chosen, 1997), pp. 163-165 (the nature and role of memes) and pp. 153-158 (memory patterns).
2. See appendix 3 "Spiritual Mapping and Community Transformation" for more complete definitions of "spiritual quest sites" and "social bondage sites."

3. Stanley Payne, *The Art of Asking Questions* (Princeton, NJ: Princeton University Press, 1980), n.p.
4. Robert Newton Peck, *A Day No Pigs Would Die* (New York: A. A. Knopf, 1994). Cited in *Reader's Digest*, "Quotable Quotes" (December 1996), p. 191.
5. A. A. Milne quoted in *Reader's Digest* (June 1994), n.p.

DRAWING CONCLUSIONS

Some Christians define spiritual mapping as the ultimate scavenger hunt. But if it were simply that, a glorified pastime for obsessive collectors, its primary practitioners would be squirrels and census takers.

To be sure, data acquisition is a part of the spiritual mapping process. But the information that is gathered is only a means to the real prize—understanding. Without this vital prize, spiritual mapping is simply religious recreation, an interesting diversion that in the end does not change anything.

Many spiritual mappers sense this danger and try to avoid it. From the outset, their research efforts are motivated by a genuine concern about the state of their communities. Ironically, it is this very concern, often urgent and consuming, that lures them into serious compromises with the truth.

Their predicament can be likened to city slickers trying to have an authentic wilderness experience. After spending the afternoon gathering wood to build a campfire, they suddenly realize that night is bearing down on them. Fearful that they will have neither the time, nor the ability, to ignite their bundles before the shadows arrive, they reach instead for kerosene lamps and propane stoves. Over dinner, they reckon that artificial light is better than no light at all.

Unfortunately, this reasoning tends to break down when carried into the spiritual realm. Here artificial light is not a handy asset, but an acute danger. Rather than enlightening spiritual travelers, it entraps them. It is nothing less than a metaphor for deception,[1] an illusion to be avoided at all costs.

The difficulty, as I noted earlier, is that many Christians get impatient, even panicky, when confronted with encroaching spiritual darkness. Some want a resolution to the problems engulfing their communities so badly they are willing to suspend critical thinking, or even invent answers. In their haste to identify and assault specific strongholds, they will embrace conclusions that, in any other field of life, even they would consider wild speculation. In the end, this rush to judgment dampens the enthusiasm of potential intercessors, squanders valuable supplies of time and money, and grants the enemy additional cover for his work.

✥

MINE THE RELEVANT FACTS
AND DISCERN THEIR COLLECTIVE
MESSAGE WITHOUT RESORTING TO
WISHFUL THINKING, THEOLOGICAL
DOGMA OR SHEER IMAGINATION.

✥

As I explained in *The Twilight Labyrinth*:

More disciplined prayer warriors have made an ally out of patience. By taking time to educate themselves about areas of concern, and then waiting on the Holy Spirit for understanding, they have learned to make accurate distinctions between *prevailing bondages* and *root bondages*.

This distinction is not always easy to make. Prevailing bondages, while visible and active, can also be thin and transitory. Like agricultural topsoil, they tend to ride the fickle winds of change—a characteristic that makes them unreliable indicators of the true nature of a stronghold. While these bondages cannot be ignored, neither should they be mistaken for the spiritual bedrock that must be broken up if territorial strongholds are to succumb to the Gospel. Only by plowing beneath the surface of a given society are we able to confront the root bondages that control it.[2]

Getting to the bottom of things takes time. You must first mine the relevant facts, and then discern their collective message—without resorting to wishful thinking, theological dogma or sheer imagination. It is no easy task.

Even the revelation of the Holy Spirit must be processed with care. As I pointed out in chapter 8, it is easy to mistake research leads for research conclusions. Most of the time God is simply trying to direct your attention to people, places or events that hold important secrets. Instead of publishing these subjective impressions, you should validate and supplement them with objective evidence (something you will surely find if the Holy Spirit has nudged you). Ignore this advice, and you will only confuse your audience. The revelation you have received has been accurate, but it is also incomplete. Admiring individual puzzle pieces is not the same as seeing a full and finished picture. As Mary so ably demonstrated (see Luke 2:19), momentous truths can be pondered, and even treasured, in the heart until it is time to bring them forth.

Analysis, while it sounds complicated, is simply a matter of examining your information in the light of biblical principles and a few standard rules of interpretation. Add a measure of prayer and common sense to this process and you're in business.

REVIEWING THE RULES OF INTERPRETATION

The line between faith and superstition is exceedingly narrow and often crossed. Common violators include counselors, evangelists, intercessors and researchers —people who carry great burdens with minimal assistance.

A vintage example of this sort of thing is found in the Jewish Talmud. It takes the form of advice to householders who suspect, but cannot document, the presence of evil spirits.

> If you want to discover demons, take sifted ashes and sprinkle them around your bed. In the morning, you will see something like the footprints of a cock. If you want to see them [demons], take the after-birth of a black she-cat, the firstborn of a firstborn, roast it in the fire and grind it to powder, and then put some in your eye...[3]

More recently, philosopher of science Hilary Putnam offered his own tongue-in-cheek "demon theory." The hypothesis, which I referred to in *The Twilight Labyrinth,* is this: A demon will appear before your eyes if you put a flour bag on your head and rap a table 16 times in quick succession. Putnam calls this Demon Theory No. 16. Demon Theory No. 17 is the same, except there have to be 17 raps, and so on. The list of theories is endless.

IF SOME CHRISTIANS ARE MISLED IN THEIR WHOLE-SALE DISTRUST OF THE SUPERNATURAL, OTHERS ERR IN THEIR WHOLESALE APPROPRIATION OF IT.

Putnam's point, of course, is that you have to be selective about the theories you quarry. It is possible to spend a lifetime digging into implausible theories and get nowhere. The trick is to winnow out the "possibly true" hypotheses from those not worth bothering with. If some Christians are misled in their wholesale distrust of the supernatural, others err in their wholesale appropriation of it. This is particularly true of certain "demon chasers" who all too often define the modern spiritual warfare movement.[4]

ALWAYS TEST YOUR ASSUMPTIONS

To a certain extent, anyone who has mastered a particular culture has applied the rules of analysis to do so. Observing and listening lead to *inferences,* a process that can involve reasoning from evidence (what we perceive) or from premises (what we assume). While our perceptions and assumptions are often correct, they can just as easily be mistaken. And wrong assumptions, as I noted in chapter 3, have a nasty habit of leading to wrong conclusions. The only sure protection is for us to test our assumptions before we get too attached to them.

For example, if we want to "prove," that Hollywood is the moral trendsetter for America, then we will have to compare its influence with that of cities like San Francisco, New Orleans and Washington, D.C. If we want to argue that the alcoholism plaguing Native peoples in Canada is the legacy of ancient spiritual pacts, we must first examine several viable counter-arguments—including the suggestion that the problem stems from modern social injustice.[5]

Some assumptions sound good until they are subjected to thoughtful scrutiny. In a letter to the editor of a South Carolina newspaper, a reader wrote: "I am in favor of daylight savings time. I have planted a vegetable garden for many years and find it does much better with that extra hour of sunlight every day!"[6] What this reader (and countless other casual observers) overlooked was the fact that daylight savings time does not yield any additional sunshine. A faulty assumption had gone unchecked for years.

The inhabitants of Paris made a similar mistake in A.D. 582 when the skies released a crimson rain over the city. Many terrified residents saw this "blood" as a sign from heaven and prostrated themselves before God. No one knew that the true cause of this odd event was the sirocco wind that sometimes blows from the Sahara across the Mediterranean into Europe. Laden with a fine red dust from the desert interior, it had dyed the rain that fell on Paris.[7]

In more recent times, I have heard spiritual warriors declare their community to be a "stronghold of Leviathan" or "bound by a python spirit." Others have taken it upon themselves to "sever ley lines" or "cancel the assignments" of resident demonic powers. The underlying assumptions, most of them untested, are as varied as the terminology.

To be honest, I find the certitude behind many of these statements a bit unsettling. If experience teaches us anything, it is that conclusions about spiritual conflicts and powers are best announced with tentativeness. We should always be ready to set them forth, but, we should be equally prepared to reopen the case if and when new evidence presents itself. Rigid assessments of prevailing strongholds and hasty declarations of spiritual victory are proven precursors to self-deception.

START WITH SIMPLE EXPLANATIONS

When looking for explanations it is tempting to expect, or even want, added complexity and drama. This is especially true when the problems confronting our community are severe. If these difficulties can be attributed to either natural phenomena, human choices or demonic activity, we prefer the demons. Where there is a selection of infernal perpetrators, we favor fallen archangels over garden-variety fiends—especially if they have malevolent sounding names like Beelzebub, Belial or Leviathan.

This same observation applies to troubled locations. Many spiritual mappers are quick to conclude that a roadway congested with shrines and temples is evidence of an underlying ley line. What they often overlook is the fact that it may once have been the *only* road in town. In neighborhoods cluttered with brothels and adult bookstores, spiritual strongholds are seen as a cause rather than a result. Zoning regulations are deemed all but irrelevant.

This is unfortunate, for, as most experienced researchers will tell you, the simplest explanation that accords with the evidence is usually the best. You should not resort to novel assumptions or hypotheses except when necessary.

"If," as William Poundstone writes in *Labyrinths of Reason*, "a footprint in the snow *might* be explained by a bear, and *might* be explained by a previously undiscovered manlike creature, the bear hypothesis is favored." This is not simply a matter of choosing the less sensational explanation. "One favors bears over abominable snowmen only when the evidence (such as a half-melted footprint) is so deficient that both the bear and the yeti theory account for it equally well."[8]

Sometimes the best alternative *is* sensational. UFO landings, for example, offered a more plausible explanation at one time for Britain's mysterious crop circles than an opposing theory that vast herds of hedgehogs had trampled them out. When simple explanations fail to account for certain realities, researchers must be prepared to migrate to more extravagant hypotheses. Narrow-mindedness is no less damaging than credulity. Misplaced skepticism in the past, for example, has diverted attention from realities like the true shape of the earth and the role of microorganisms in causing disease. Extraordinary claims require extraordinary proof, but sometimes the evidence we seek is nestled right under our noses. As Sherlock Holmes observed, "There is nothing more deceptive than an obvious fact."[9]

NEVER INTERPRET THE WHOLE ON THE BASIS OF THE PARTICULAR

Amateur analysts violate this rule with regularity, the most common reason being simple laziness. They are like accountants who build company budgets through extrapolated formulas rather than line-item research. In the end, speed is more important than accuracy, information more valuable than truth. Their objective is not to change anything, merely to report statistics or a story. Why gather multiple accounts when one will do?

Over the years I have watched many preoccupied Westerners

visit China with hopes of contacting the underground Church. Crammed into small homes, they listen wide-eyed as one or two believers unfold the latest tales of blessing and persecution. On the basis of these brief encounters, they form sweeping conclusions about life and faith in the People's Republic. No effort is made to determine if their informants are balanced and knowledgeable, or whether they have any vested interests. Their perception of the "facts" in China is colored entirely by the particular biases of one or two individuals.

One Oxford lecturer back in the 1960s was fond of telling his students that "facts mean nothing." What did he mean by this statement? Simply that a fact, unless it is related to some other facts, or until its significance is pointed out, means surprisingly little.

The importance of related facts cannot be overstated. Each fact or statistic, before it can become truly meaningful, must be viewed in context. If research reveals there are 10 New Age groups in your town, your immediate reaction may be one of great concern. This concern will likely be mitigated, however, by the subsequent report that nine of these organizations were in the community 30 years ago. The addition of one group in a 30-year span is hardly an indicator that New Age cults (at least in your community) are spreading like wildfire. Further relief is provided by the fact that 200 Christian churches are now active in the city—an increase of 40 percent over the same three decades.

A wise man once told his students, "When you have enough nothings, their sum is something." A particular piece of information might be meaningless on its own, but when it is combined with other data new possibilities emerge. Puzzle pieces being fit together into a scene offer a good example of this process. Individual pieces may not "say" anything at first, but when they are brought into alignment with related segments, the "message" can be dazzling. The late Swedish economist, Gunnar Myrdahl, was among the first modern scholars to draw attention to this phenomenon. While acknowledging that facts do not always speak for themselves, the 1974 Nobel Prize winner insisted they did have a means of communication. When relevant information is brought together, he declared, "Facts kick!"

LETTING FACTS KICK

At some point in your research, a certain combination of facts is going to confront you. This may occur during the course of an interview, or as you review a particular combination of data overlays. Whenever it happens, you will feel as though you have been kicked in the ribs without warning. All of a sudden, you will discover new properties in data scenes and relationships. Things will make sense, suspicions will be confirmed, fresh concepts and propositions will emerge.

The revelatory scenarios are virtually limitless. In one situation you might perceive the connection between a traumatic historical event and the onset of spirit appeasement or humanistic philosophy. On another occasion the insight might be related to a specific pattern of adaptive deceptions. On yet another it might confirm the identity of a person or institution that God is using to prepare the community for change. The important thing is that the correlations are unforced. There is no human manipulation, no artificial connections.

When facts start kicking they will draw you to obvious and compelling conclusions. These may be grand, climactic solutions, or a chain-reaction of new patterns and linkages. Both qualify as authentic analytical breakthroughs. Your response should be one of thanksgiving to God, not only for His faithfulness to you and your community but also for His willingness to partner with human beings.

Recognizing spiritual patterns and continuums is the very essence of spiritual mapping. No report is complete until it explains why and how human misery is perpetuated in the community and why there is ongoing resistance to the gospel and its messengers. If you cannot elucidate these matters, it is time to get back to work.

WEIGHING AND VALIDATING DATA

In the process of assigning value to certain pieces of information, there are at least four criteria that need to be considered. These include:

1. The known relevance of the information
2. The integrity of your source
3. The level of confirmation
4. The availability of scriptural validation

While these standards do not bestow automatic significance upon any datum, they can raise critical suspicions. Taken together they represent an important analytical filter.

Known Relevance

The first thing you must determine is whether a given fact or statement matches the essential elements of your mission. Since your goal is to investigate obstacles to revival in your community, you certainly don't need to be collecting recipes or weather statistics. Such things will only clutter your files. If you are unsure of a datum's relevance, place it in a tickler file until you can conduct a further review. Conclusions should also be checked against this criterion. Your draft report ought to have wide margins where you can scrawl the question "Significance?" next to any paragraph where it is not readily apparent.

Integrity of Source

Another prime consideration is the honesty and reliability of the people who provide you with information. What is their track record or reputation? Do they have any vested interests? Are they people pleasers? If you do not know the answers to these questions it behooves you to seek them out. They are every bit as important as the original data. It is equally important to determine whether the information you have received from an interview is a statement of fact or opinion. Both can be useful, but you should recognize and acknowledge the difference.

Level of Confirmation

In the book of Proverbs at least three passages point out the wisdom found in a multitude of counselors (see 11:14; 15:22; 24:6). When you hear the same thing from many sources, there is a strong likelihood that the information is accurate. You also reap the benefit of varied perspectives (much like the Synoptic Gospels). This adds rich detail and texture to your story. On the flip side of this equation, a diminished list of respondents will cause your vision and confidence to suffer. Theories built around solitary informants are the riskiest of all. Always remember this simple admonition: The fewer the sources, the greater the caution.

Scriptural Validation

This final criterion is based on a single question: Does a particular fact or conclusion conflict with the record or principles of Scripture? If it does, toss it out immediately and move on. If you are not sure, get some theological counsel from your pastor or another skilled Bible teacher.

In the end, there is always the possibility that God's Word may have little or nothing to say on the subject. Should this be the case, it is best to present your information in a manner and tone that is free of dogmatism. When scriptural support *is* available, be sure to insert the appropriate references into your report.

STAYING PRACTICAL (CLOSE TO THE ROAD)

The results of a spiritual mapping campaign are more closely related to an intelligence report than a scholarly paper. And that is as it should be. Your goal, after all, is not merely to learn about your community but to take appropriate action. To reach this goal you need to stay focused—and practical.

The same questions that provided a framework for your data acquisition (see chapter 6) should now guide the analysis phase of your project. In case you have forgotten these core questions, I'll list them again.

1. What is wrong with my community?
2. Where did the problem come from?
3. What can be done to change things?

Your answers to these questions should be long on facts and response strategies and short on interesting but unrelated theories. When readers evaluate the contents of your report, they will ask two things: Does it matter? and Is it practical? As an electrical engineer once observed, "The biggest waterfall in the world won't run an airplane."

While speculative theories may be good entertainment they are lousy motivators. If you want people to act, you must give them substance. If you want their actions to be productive, you must give them substance that has been tested. Change will not occur until people are convinced there is a need for it. They must then be persuaded that there is a viable alternative and that they are capable of carrying it out.

HIDDEN DANGERS

Spiritual mapping research is inherently dangerous. Not only will you have to contend with long hours, unsavory neighborhoods and hostile respondents, but you may also confront a series of demonic roadblocks. The consequences can range from inexplicable equipment failure to emotional depression and physical illness or assault. Besides coping with overt harassment, you must be on constant guard against subtle deceptions that can, and often do, derail the best of intentions.

When it comes to war, anticipation is better than reaction. This is also true in spiritual mapping. You cannot always prevent things from going wrong, but you can be prepared for them when they do You can also avoid certain snares if you know where to look—and it is to this end that I have included the following sections.

❧

ONE THE GREATEST DANGERS ASSOCIATED WITH SPIRITUAL MAPPING IS EXCLUSIVITY—AN ELITIST "IN THE KNOW" ATTITUDE WHERE NO ONE ELSE SEES THINGS QUITE AS CLEARLY OR PROFOUNDLY AS YOU DO.

❧

THE EXCLUSIVIST SYNDROME: CLAIMING "SPECIAL VISION"
One of the greatest dangers associated with spiritual mapping is the potential for mysticism and exclusivity. A common symptom of this syndrome is an elitist "in the know" attitude, a sense that

no one else sees things quite as clearly or profoundly as you do. While this condition may not seem serious, it is capable of leading you into a narrow, isolated place where you can be easily deceived.

So how do you avoid the exclusivist syndrome? The first and most important step is to remember why you are doing investigative research. Is it not to welcome the presence of the Holy Spirit into your community? And does this not require a humble and open heart? The apostle James asks:

> Who is wise and understanding among you? Let him show it by his good life, by deeds done in the humility that comes from wisdom (Jas. 3:13).

Other protective measures include accountability (independent cross-checks can save your life) and practicality. Does it bother you when others question your revelations or conclusions? This may be a sign you have lost your balance. After all, nothing is more irritating to a fanatic than common sense.

THE QUICKSAND OF CARELESSNESS: IGNORING RESEARCH BOUNDARIES

Another common snare faced by spiritual mappers is overconfidence. Having embarked on a good cause, there is a sense that nothing bad can happen to you, that you are invulnerable to powers and circumstances that would normally inflict great harm. In time this overconfidence leads to carelessness. Research activities are pursued across dangerous boundaries. You make plans to attend, or even participate in, various religious rituals—all without checking in with the Holy Spirit or marshaling proper prayer support. At other times you review "how to" techniques in books dealing with forbidden occult subjects.

The surest way to avoid unhealthy and unnecessary detours is to stick with your mission and your Master. Human presumption is among the most common attractors to the demonic. The only antidote is thorough repentance followed by habitual submission to the will of God. As I noted in *The Twilight Labyrinth*, walking in obedience makes us safer by limiting enemy inroads into our lives. It also allows God to defend His own purposes. While this support does not prevent the devil from taking his best shot (witness Elijah, Mordecai and Paul), it does make us more difficult targets.[10]

THE RESEARCH CAROUSEL: NOT KNOWING WHEN TO STOP
If the enemy cannot prevent you from starting a project, he will surely endeavor to keep you from finishing. He does this by fascinating you with the twists and turns of the spiritual dimension—and especially with himself. And it works! As Leon Uris observed in *Redemption*, "Often we have no time for our friends but all the time in the world for our enemies."[11] The devil leads us to no destination, only on an endless journey up blind alleys and intellectual cul-de-sacs. He traps us in esoterica.

Projects that are always under revision, but never acted upon, are like a long wooden bridge being built across a river. By the time the bridge is completed to the far shore, the floorboards first laid down are rotting. By that time, those near the middle of the bridge must be replaced, and so on. It never is completely ready for use, and it never will be in spite of the hard work that has gone into it.

While spiritual mapping research is a lengthy and detailed pursuit, it does have an end. But to succeed, you must love this end more than the process of reaching it. Should you find your passion for evangelism has cooled, ask God for a fresh revelation of His heart. And pay attention! He just might do this through your research.

A CHECKLIST OF PROTECTIVE MEASURES
There are several other things you and your team can do to main-

tain a hedge against the enemy. Although each of these measures is uncomplicated, they will only work if they are put into practice.

• Remain accountable

The purpose of accountability is to establish guardrails to keep us out of trouble and a safety tether in case we stumble into it. We submit one to another for the same reason that hikers are encouraged to check in with park rangers before heading into wilderness areas. Knowing someone is watching out for us affords both protection and confidence. (See Gal. 6:2; Heb. 13:17.)

• Maintain a devotional life

When you head into an arduous assignment, it is important to stay spiritually fit. However the enemy may roar on the field, it is what God says during your moments with Him that counts. Apart from intimacy with God, you can too easily end up like the spies in Canaan who saw only giants and grasshoppers. (See Psalms 1:2,3; 119:97,98,105.)

• Recruit prayer support

Some ministry assignments call for added measures, and spiritual mapping is surely one of these. Accordingly, it is a good idea to recruit a team of personal intercessors who will hold you up before God in prayer. (These are separate from the team's intercessory unit.) Be sure to keep them well fed with information. (See Eph. 6:18; 1 Tim. 2:1.)

Once you have completed your initial research, including data acquisition and analysis, it is time to deliver the results.

NOTES

1. George Otis, Jr., *The Twilight Labyrinth*, (Grand Rapids: Chosen, 1997), pp. 71-74.
2. Ibid., p. 227.
3. The Talmud, Berachot 6a.
4. Otis, Jr., *The Twilight Labyrinth*, p. 65.
5. In this case the truth embraces both explanations.
6. Contributed by Frederick Gales, *Reader's Digest*, (December 1996), p. 154.
7. While some will argue that God can use naturally occurring phenomena to accomplish His purposes, this misses my point. The issue here is the Parisians' mistaken, and no doubt quickly formed, assumption that the rain falling over their city was blood.
8. William Poundstone, *Labyrinths of Reason* (New York: Doubleday, 1988), p. 53.
9. Otis, Jr., *The Twilight Labyrinth*, p. 66.
10. Ibid., pp. 246, 247.
11. Leon Uris, *Redemption* (New York: HarperCollins Publications, 1996), n.p. Cited in *Reader's Digest* (June 1997), n.p.

Chapter 10

⤦

BRIEFING
THE TROOPS

Now that you have assessed the spiritual dynamics at work in your community, it is time to report your findings. This may seem anticlimactic after months of intriguing fieldwork and divine revelation, but it is critical to the success of your mission. If no one knows about or listens to your conclusions, the long days of research and analysis will have been an exercise in futility. To capitalize on your labors, you must transition from investigating hidden problems to selling others on the need for action.

Of course, you may have already used your discoveries to stoke the boilers of motivated community intercessors. As I noted in chapters 2 and 3, these nuggets of intelligence, offered as progressive revelation, can be highly effective in sustaining fervent intercession.

This said, there will come a time when it is appropriate to present these revelations as part of a complete package. God can use your comprehensive report to draw others into the battle for the community. People may well have heard bits and pieces of your discovery, but they will not commit themselves to serious action until they see the "big picture."

Ask the Holy Spirit to help you in this task. The same prayer that brought about the completion of your report will enable you sell it. God is no slacker, and He is especially motivated to see that your findings (His revelations) are disseminated to people who will do something with them.

The packaging, tone and timing of your presentation are also important, and it is to these matters that we now turn our attention.

WRAPPING IT UP: PACKAGING IS IMPORTANT!

A quality presentation is important for several reasons. Among the more obvious of these is the need to connect with your audience. If your report is not relevant or readable, if it lacks a standardized, user-friendly format, people will simply not bother with it. And if this is not reason enough to commit to a clean and polished product, remember that your work is a reflection of who you are—not to mention a very real offering to the Lord Jesus.

GENERAL FORMAT

The general format of a report is like a blueprint. It is what permits you to maintain control over your project during the construction phase. It also determines what the final product will look like.

In chapter 4, we reviewed several types of spiritual mapping products. These ranged from non-standardized profiles and briefings to highly structured reports. The latter, which sustain fervent intercession through progressive revelation, require researchers to answer certain questions in proper sequence. Although this may seem arbitrary, it is actually a reflection of the rhythm of heaven. God has procedures—and they show up everywhere. Remember the farmer who hopes to harvest a bumper crop? His procedures are simple but rigid. He must first till the soil and then plant, fertilize and irrigate his seeds. He is not free to ignore a particular task or to reverse the sequence in which they are performed.

A QUALITY PRESENTATION IS IMPORTANT.
YOUR WORK IS A REFLECTION OF WHO YOU ARE—
NOT TO MENTION A VERY REAL OFFERING
TO THE LORD JESUS.

The other benefit of an ordered or standardized layout is that similarly designed products lend themselves to comparative analyses. As I mentioned in chapter 4, this is particularly important in the detection of regional strongholds or spiritual patterns.

Having established that your final report needs structure, the next step is to review the desired blueprint and evaluate basic construction techniques.

Chapter Contents and Order

The configuration of your report—its table of contents if you like—should correspond with the research categories (such as prevailing social bondages and the potential for spiritual breakthroughs) outlined in chapter 6. You will want to devote one chapter to each category, with content comprised of answers to the discovery questions contained in appendix 2 of "Practical Resources." Your chapters should also include a cogent summary or conclusion. (Appendix 1 provides excellent chapter subtitles.) After you have completed the main body of your report (the only section that needs to be standardized), you can add as many special features and appendices as you like.

Readability

Since most people won't stick with a publication they can't easily read, it is important that your writing style be lucid and logical. While many individuals think they can turn a word, few actually have the talent to sustain a reader's interest. If you are not a particularly good writer, turn the task over to someone who is. A competent editor can help make your report user-friendly.

As you write, always keep your audience in mind. Remember whom you are trying to communicate with.

While your readers will not be children, neither are they likely to be scientists or professors. A robust vocabulary and literary sophistication are assets only if they are appreciated by your audience. Your goal is to communicate with your readers, not to dazzle them.

Finally, don't be verbose. In the art of report writing, less is often more. If you are confused about what to include, consider this helpful rule of thumb: If an incident or detail does not contribute to your stated purpose, you should leave it out, no matter how interesting it may be.

Using Graphic Inserts

Graphics such as charts and photographs will greatly enhance the impact of your final report—so feel free to use them. Just remember that it is possible to have too much of a good thing. If you insert an overwhelming number of graphic devices into the main body of your work, readability will be compromised.

One good idea is to insert timelines and data overlays in your report. These acetate sheets can be employed for illustrative purposes within a particular chapter or included in a more comprehensive appendix. Wherever they end up, your readers will appreciate the chance to see your conclusions, not just read them.

INSURING A READY AUDIENCE

Once your written report is complete, it is time to formally present it to your commissioning authority. If you have maintained regular contact throughout the campaign, this event should be eagerly anticipated. It is like coming to the end of a good book. Monthly briefings are the chapters that provide progressive revelation. By the time people have attended 10 to 15 of these sessions they should be familiar with the plot. The only thing left is the dramatic conclusion.

You can leave it up to your pastor or ministry leader to decide if they want an executive briefing before the report is made public. If they do, you might want to prepare a set of charts or overheads to enhance your presentation. Short videos and slide shows can also be effective.

Whether or not you elect to use visual aides, be sure to provide each member of the leadership team with a personalized copy of the final report. This personalization should include an addressed cover letter that expresses appreciation for their prayer and (if appropriate) financial support and a summary of any follow-up actions you would like them to approve.

Your actual presentation should be brief and to the point. Thirty to forty-five minutes is about as long as you want to go. Any longer and you run the risk of losing people. Confine your remarks to project highlights and recommendations. If the leadership team wants to ask specific questions, let them be the ones to extend the meeting.

Lastly, you and your leadership team should understand that no spiritual mapping report will ever be truly finished. This is because communities are, by their very nature, dynamic. People are always making new choices. Some of these choices are good (such as Nineveh's response to the warnings of Jonah), while others are lamentable (such as Solomon's decision to take foreign wives). Given this reality, your "final report" is best viewed as an initial status report that must be updated and amended on an annual basis. Spiritual mapping is not a one-time activity but a constant companion in the quest to reach your community for Christ.

EXPANDING YOUR RESPONSE TEAM

If your research has been part of a citywide effort involving multiple partners, you will eventually need to fit your conclusions into the larger puzzle. This is where things start to get exciting—if the collective investigation has been well coordinated and thorough. Allow God to speak to you during this process. He will not only reveal His feelings for your community; He will also transplant these feelings directly into your own heart. He will also offer up strategies for responding to the challenges your research has surfaced.

As you make the transition from research to response, look for ways to collaborate with other local ministries. Partnership is God's favored methodology, especially when the task is too large for any one group to handle effectively. Even if you are involved with a denomination or mission agency, your primary loyalty and responsibility should be to the community where God has placed you. Partnerships not only make practical sense; they are a powerful witness to a selfish and lonely world.

If you would like to develop or expand a community partnership but are unsure how to go about it, there are several organizations willing to help. Depending on your level of need, they can provide assistance through books and videos, online services, regional seminars or on-site coaching. (A more comprehensive listing of these services and the organizations that provide them may be found in the "Practical Resources" section at the back of this book.)

Whether you are looking for organizational referrals or simply trying to identify other spiritual mappers in your area, a smart first step is to contact The Sentinel Group. As a pioneer of the modern spiritual mapping movement, Sentinel has developed an excellent network of contacts around the world. The ministry also operates an international E-mail list called the Mapper's Forum that provides news and networking options for spiritual mappers. If Sentinel doesn't have the answer you're seeking, they can probably put you in touch with someone who does. Other groups with global reach include the World Prayer Center, Harvest Evangelism International and Hispanic International Ministries. If you are pursuing community transformation in the United States, your best bets are The Sentinel Group, Mission America and CitiReach International—an offshoot of DAWN Ministries that hopes to have 12 to 20 full-time consultants deployed by January 2003.

DROPPING THE PAYLOAD

The officers shall say to the army: "Has anyone built a new house and not dedicated it? Let him go home, or he may die in battle and someone else may dedicate it. Has anyone planted a vineyard and not begun to enjoy it? Let him go home, or he may die in battle and someone else enjoy it" (Deut. 20:5,6).

While the focus of this book has been on community transformation, many of us are "going to battle" outside our own city. Often our chosen mission is directed at the prevention of national self-destruction or the liberation of far-flung peoples from spiritual darkness. These objectives are both admirable and biblical, but they do not release us from the responsibility of first "dedicating our own land" and "reaping our own vineyards." Though we have been called to be World Christians, we must not forget that our home community is an integral part of the world we must reach (see Luke 24:47; Acts 1:8).

Satan often takes advantage of our "love leaps" to seize control of local streets, schools and businesses. If his occupation goes unchallenged, the spiritual and social walls of our community eventually fall into disrepair. When this happens our only hope is that God will raise up a modern Nehemiah to help us reclaim our heritage.

The road to community transformation is not an easy one. Those who make the journey must have patience, focus and commitment. They must be prepared to give ample time to uncover problems and to identify solutions. Then, when their understanding has ripened, they must be prepared to act—or as they say in the military, drop the payload. As I observed in chapter 4, communities do not change merely because we have become aware of the nature and origins of spiritual strongholds; they change because revived believers enter into fervent and united prayer.

So what kind of prayers should you offer? Other than petitioning the Lord to stimulate an appetite for the things that attract His presence—namely humility, unity, holiness and prayer—the Bible offers no set strategies. Every situation is different. God may direct one group of believers to hold all-night prayer vigils (Cali, Colombia), while another is instructed to preach to community leaders about idolatry (Umuahia, Nigeria). It all depends on God's assessment of local circumstances. There is no one-size-fits-all approach to spiritual warfare strategy or methodology.

❧

THE FOCAL POINT OF OUR PRAYERS SHOULD BE GOD,
NOT THE DEVIL. RAILING AT THE ENEMY IS RECKLESS
AND IMMATURE. IT IS ALSO DANGEROUS.

❧

Having said this, the Bible does set forth principles to help insure the success of any approach God might commend. These principles include maintaining a clean heart (see Luke 11:34-36), walking in a spirit of humility and dependence (see Luke 12:35,36; Jas. 4:6), and making our requests in faith (see Matt. 21:22). If we want to evangelize people whose minds have been blinded by demonic deceptions (see 2 Cor. 4:4), we must begin by asking God to bind the strongman so that we can spoil his goods (see Mark 3:27). We are not requesting that He save the entire community or permanently evict demonic powers when this is contrary to the will of the local populace. He simply won't answer such prayers. What He will do—and this should be the focus of our intercession—is level the playing field by temporarily lifting the logical consequences of people's misplaced choices. With their spiritual enchantment neutralized, lost men and women are suddenly able to process the gospel at a heart level. If they take advantage of this opportunity to repent of their sin, their liberation can become permanent.

The focal point of our prayers should be God, not the devil. If the evil one is to be bound, it will take divine strength to do the job. Railing at the enemy is reckless and immature. It is also dangerous. We must never forget that we are dealing with a higher dimensional being whose capabilities greatly exceed our own. Spiritual swagger and clichés mean nothing to him.

While it is true that we have been given power and authority in Christ (see Luke 10:19), this authority is not for us to use at our own initiative or discretion. It is ambassadorial authority—which means that it is to be exercised only at the Sovereign's bidding. If the task before us is a matter of simple exorcism, authorization to act has already been given (see Mark 6:7; 16:17); we have only to insure that our relationship with God is intact (see Acts 19:15,16). If, on the other hand, we are attempting to bind the influence of territorial spirits or prophesy the demise (or restoration) of political entities, we must pray until God gives the Amen.[1] When Jeremiah was appointed "to uproot and tear down, to destroy and overthrow, to build and to plant," his authority derived from the fact that God's own words had been placed in his mouth (Jer. 1:9,10).

Of course, this entire discussion presupposes that spiritual mappers will want, and even need, to respond to the things their research has uncovered. Looking reality square in the face has a way of taxing the emotions, especially if the observation has occurred over time. The apostle Paul was deeply stirred when he saw the people of Athens wholly given over to idolatry and superstition. Jesus was similarly moved when he reflected on the stubborn unbelief of Jerusalem. As the record shows, both men responded to these troubling visions by taking practical action.

In the end, there is no better therapy for an anguished spirit.

On the other hand, the surest path to misery is coming to understand one's community and then leaving it the way it is. Once the bitter truths and tormenting images are confronted, they take on a life of their own. They begin to haunt our inner world so that, in time, no daydream or vacation is undisturbed. Calling oneself a professional researcher offers no haven. The Bible gives no legitimacy to a role that permits us to merely pass on facts to intercessors and evangelists. It offers no special category that exempts us from personally reaching out to the lost.

Of course, most spiritual mappers are not looking for exemptions. Having adopted the Savior's heartbeat, they view the lost not as an evil blight on the community, but as objects of God's great and undying affection. They pray passionately because they feel passionately (see Ezek. 2:9—3:4; 3:12-15).

DOES ADOPTING HEAVEN'S POINT OF VIEW REALLY WORK? Ask Thomas Muthee who has seen his poverty-stricken, witchcraft-dominated town of Kiambu, Kenya, transformed into a model community. Ask him how it feels to pastor a church of over 5,000 in a place where, for years, people "heard the gospel, but didn't get saved."

Ask Bob Beckett who, for the past two decades, has seen his community of Hemet, California, rid of powerful gangs, numerous cults and the dubious distinction of being called the methamphetamine capital of the West Coast.

Ask Mariano Riscajché who has witnessed his town of Almolonga, Guatemala, cast off rank idolatry, crippling poverty and an alcoholism rate of nearly 100 percent. Ask him what it is like to live in a town where more than 90 percent of the population are born-again Christians.

Ask Emeka Nwankpa to describe the sensation of watching his entire kindred repudiate their 300-year association with ancestral spirits.

Ask Ruth Ruibal or Randy and Marcy MacMillan to tell you about the liberation of Cali, Colombia. Ask them what it is like to be free of the cocaine cartel, to worship in a stadium filled with over 60,000 fellow believers, to experience a season of unprecedented church growth.

The message is simple and straightforward: It is time to believe God for great things. It is time to stand up and declare that we are totally against the mentality of impossibility![2]

NOTES
1. This "Amen" is something that often comes to us in the form of appropriate instructions.
2. This declaration was first made by Guatemalan pastor Harold Caballeros at the International Congress on Prayer, Spiritual Warfare and Evangelism in Guatemala City, October 1998.

DISCOVERY QUESTIONS

This appendix contains an extended list of questions that relate to the six core categories of spiritual mapping. Although this list is not exhaustive, it should nevertheless offer a useful starting point to those who need one.

The questions listed after each subheading should be answered by *every* spiritual mapping team. To ignore them is to risk potentially serious gaps and errors in the final report. Supplementary questions found at the end of some categories should be investigated only if they are deemed relevant to local circumstances.

Since many of these questions will need to be directed toward human respondents, we have included a reminder list of the basic steps that should be taken in preparing for an interview:

1. Locate a knowledgeable source.
2. Develop an explanatory introduction.
3. Arrange for an interview.
4. Familiarize yourself with key subject matter through background research.
5. Make a list of specific questions.
6. Review the list and delete repetitive or unnecessary questions.
7. Obtain and check recording equipment.

THE STATUS OF CHRISTIANITY

SIZE AND NATURE OF THE CHURCH

- ❑ What percentage of the community considers itself Christian?
- ❑ What percentage of the community considers itself evangelical?
- ❑ How does this compare with surrounding areas?
- ❑ What is the estimated number of believers in the community?
- ❑ Which denominations (if any) predominate in the community?
- ❑ What is the average-size church (attendance-wise) in the area?
- ❑ Are there any ethnic churches in the community (e.g., Hispanic or Korean)? If so, how many and what type?
- ❑ Is the church representative of all social classes in the community?

Additional Questions

- ❑ Are most Christians in the area affiliated with denominations?
- ❑ What is the ratio of old-line churches (Pentecostal or Evangelical) to newer, independent fellowships?
- ❑ How strong is the Roman Catholic Church in the area?

HEALTH OF THE CHURCH

- ❑ Does there seem to be a genuine bond of unity among Christian churches in the community? How does this manifest itself?

❑ Are there recognized apostolic leaders in the area who have made public commitments to the land/community?

❑ If community faith was strong in the past, has this fervor grown or has it given way to a permissive, lukewarm Christianity?

❑ Are most Christians in the community familiar with the basic truths of Scripture? If not, why?

❑ Do believers in the community gather for united prayer? If so, how often do these assemblies occur?

Additional Questions

❑ What is the history of church splits in the community?

❑ What percentage of the Christian community attends church more than once a week?

❑ What percentage of the churches in the area have home-based nurture groups?

❑ How does the church spend its finances? What is the ratio of money spent on property and facilities over direct outreach programs (both in and outside of the community)?

COMMUNITY PERCEPTION

❑ How visible is the Church in the community? Have there been any recent public events like "March for Jesus"?

❑ Has the Church been hurt by scandals? Have these been local?

❑ Does the community have a sense that the Church is truly interested in its problems? If yes, what kind of programs would reinforce this idea?

❑ Is the Church seen as a relevant or outmoded institution? Who in the community see it which way?

Additional Questions

❑ What kind of church news seems to attract the most attention?

EVANGELISTIC ACTIVITY AND PROGRESS

❑ Is this an area where the gospel has never taken root, or is it part of a "Bible Belt"?

❑ What percentage of the community has been reached with the gospel?

❑ Is the rate of church growth in the community consistent with general population growth? Is it higher or lower?

❑ Have all geographical sectors of the community been evangelized? If not, which ones have been missed and why?

❑ Are there specific social groups in the community that have been under-evangelized? If so, which ones and why?

❑ What type of outreach programs predominate in the community?

❑ Which of these (if any) seem to be effective? Which methodologies are ineffective and why?

PREVAILING SOCIAL BONDAGES

CONDITIONS OF PAIN

❑ Other than self-inflicted pain (e.g., alcohol and drug abuse), what is the most prevalent form of suffering in the community?

❑ Why is this particular condition so prevalent?

❑ What other kinds of pain exist within the community (e.g., injustice, poverty, discrimination, disease)?

❑ How widespread are these problems?

❑ How long have these problems existed within the community? When did they begin and *why*?

❑ Is there is a tormenting condition that is unique in either type or magnitude? How is this explained?

Additional Questions

❑ How do the conditions of pain in your community compare to those in surrounding areas?

STRUCTURAL DISINTEGRATION

❑ What influences and/or values have traditionally represented stabilizing factors in the community?

❑ Have these influences and/or values lost potency in recent years? If so, how much and why?

❑ What are the evidences of family unit disintegration in the community (e.g., divorce, spousal and child abuse)?

❑ What are the evidences of governmental disintegration in the community (e.g., corruption, partisanship)?

- ❑ What are the evidences of business disintegration in the community (e.g., layoffs, budget deficits)?
- ❑ What are the evidences of educational disintegration in the community (e.g., behavioral problems, low test scores)?

DESTRUCTIVE VICES

- ❑ What is the extent of drug and alcohol abuse within the community?
- ❑ Is pornography rampant in the community? What forms does it take (e.g., adult bookstores and clubs, phone or cybersex, child pornography)?
- ❑ Is casual sex prevalent? Is it acceptable? Is there a prostitution problem?
- ❑ What is the present status of homosexuality in the community?
- ❑ Are there other unique or associated forms of vice in the community?

Additional Questions

- ❑ Is there legalized gambling? If so, what form does it take? How many people are involved?
- ❑ Is there a significant number of nightclubs and dance halls in the area?

TROUBLING TRENDS

- ❑ What new or revitalized forms is sin taking in the community (i.e., nature worship, cybersex, designer drugs)?

❑ Is there a new willingness in the community to accept/adopt broader social limits (i.e., alternative lifestyles, abortion, teen sex)?

❑ What, if any, role does the media have in promoting spiritual darkness in the community?

❑ Are there any new alliances forming between groups or institutions that wish to promote unrighteousness?

❑ Is there a new militancy on the part of sinners? If so, what are some recent examples of this?

❑ Are there any serious physical and/or psychological side-effects associated with new societal indulgences (e.g., AIDS)?

WORLDVIEWS AND ALLEGIANCES

PREDOMINANT PHILOSOPHIES AND RELIGIONS

❑ Do most people in the community believe in God? How do they define Him?

❑ Do most people in the community believe in the devil (or demons)? How do they define him/them?

❑ Other than Christianity, what major religions are represented in the community (e.g., Islam, Mormonism, Judaism, Buddhism)?

❑ How many people are involved with these other religions?

❑ Are recent immigrants swelling the ranks of these other faiths? If yes, where are they coming from and what religions do they follow?

❑ Have local ethnic communities (e.g., African American, Chinese, Korean, Hispanic) adopted any of these religions?

❏ What is the size and influence of the New Age Movement?

❏ Are there important religious centers in the area? What is their declared purpose? Is there reason to believe they are more than what they seem?

❏ What are the predominant secular philosophies in the area (e.g., humanism, rationalism, materialism)? What is their level of influence?

Additional Questions

❏ Other than Mormonism, what pseudo-Christian cults are active in the community (e.g., Jehovah's Witnesses)?

❏ Is there a sizable Jewish population in the community? Are they religious? If so, are they orthodox, liberal or mystical (kabbala)?

❏ Are there Native American peoples in the area? Are they religious?

❏ Are non-Indian peoples being drawn into Native American religion? If so, how is this occurring?

❏ Are there any African or Caribbean religions operating in the community (e.g., voodoo or Santeria)?

SIGNIFICANT EVENTS AND PRACTICES

❏ How exactly do people show their religious or philosophical devotion (e.g., worship services, religious pilgrimages)?

❏ Are these merely cultural reflexes, or is there evidence that people are genuinely serious about their beliefs?

❏ Other than those associated with Christianity, what religious holidays (if any) are observed in the community?

❑ Has the community taken any steps to reaffirm ancient spiritual pacts or practices?

❑ Are there any sacred ritual sites in the area? If so, what are they? Are they still in use?

❑ Are pagan rituals or secular philosophies being practiced and/or encouraged in community schools?

❑ Are there any known secret societies operating in the community (e.g., Masonic lodges, witchcraft covens)? What is known about the practices of such groups?

❑ What dates and times are significant to local religious groups? Why?

Additional Questions

❑ What (if any) Christo-pagan celebrations are held in the community? What rituals are associated with these events?

❑ What information (if any) is available on New Age meditation retreats or Native American vision quests in the area?

❑ Are there any magazines or journals that describe important religious activities, events or sites in the area?

INFLUENTIAL DEITIES AND ROLE MODELS

❑ Who are some of the most influential human figures in the community (living or dead)?

❑ Who commands the minds and affection of the youth in the community? Are they positive role models? Are they linked to a non-Christian religion or philosophy?

❑ Do any noteworthy spiritual or philosophical gurus

reside/practice in the area? What kind of following do they have?

❑ What gods are worshipped in non-Christian circles? Are they developed personalities or abstractions?

❑ Do local peoples worship/fear any gods or deities that are associated with particular locations (e.g., neighborhoods, homes, mountains)?

❑ Is there any inferential or oblique worship of ancient deities through community customs or places names?

❑ Are there overt strongholds of idolatry in the community (e.g., Hindu temples or ancestral shrines)?

❑ Are there more ambiguous centers of idolatry in the community (e.g., athletic arenas, shopping malls, dance clubs)? Who or what is worshiped in these places?

SPIRITUAL OPPOSITION

HUMAN GROUPS AND PERSONALITIES

❑ Is there tangible opposition to the gospel in the community?

❑ Has this opposition been long-standing or is it a recent development?

❑ Is this opposition formal and organized or merely attitudinal?

❑ Has any legislation been passed that impinges on Christian values and/or practices? Is any being proposed?

❑ Do any area politicians, bureaucrats, judges or police officials go out of their way to obstruct the gospel? If so, what is motivating their behavior?

❑ Has there been any public mockery of Christianity?

❑ Has there been any physical persecution of Christians? Has there been any damage to Christian property?

❑ What kind of opposition (if any) has come from the members or leaders of other religious groups? Which individuals or groups are involved?

❑ What kind of opposition (if any) has come from militant secularists? Which individuals or groups are involved?

❑ What kind of opposition (if any) has come from militant social groups (e.g., homosexuals or radical feminists)? Who is involved?

❑ Is there any verifiable evidence that local witches or shamans have placed curses on Christian personnel, property or activities?

❑ Have local Christian leaders, either as individuals or as a group, publicly opposed evangelism and/or fresh moves of the Holy Spirit?

❑ Is there any evidence of new or ungodly alliances that may be forming against the cause of Christ?

DEMONIC POWERS

❑ Are there any known regional or territorial deities that would oppose the advance of the gospel?

❑ Are there certain areas in the community where occultism or other spiritual bondages have truncated church growth?

❑ Is there evidence of increased spiritual opposition during or immediately following religious festivals or ceremonies?

❑ Do certain neighborhoods, religious groups or ethnic

communities seem to contain a disproportionate number of demonized people?

Additional Questions

❏ Have there been instances where Christian workers have suffered inexplicable illnesses, financial reversals or accidents after preaching against a particular form of idolatry?

❏ Have intercessors or evangelists suffered bouts of depression after witnessing or engaging in warfare prayer around known spiritual strongholds?

❏ Are there certain natural sites or buildings that are widely believed to be haunted or demonized? Has this prevented the gospel from taking root in the area?

THE EVOLUTION OF CURRENT CIRCUMSTANCES

ROOT FACTORS AND EVENTS

❏ Who were the original settlers of this region?

❏ Where did they come from and when?

❏ What was their primary religious worldview? Who did they worship?

❏ What is known about their motives for coming to the region?

❏ Did the region's pioneers experience any recorded traumas? If so, what was the nature of these experiences?

❏ Did they attempt to resolve any of these traumas by entering into pacts with spirits? If so, how and when did this occur?

❑ Is there any historical evidence that their allegiance to these spirits or deities was formalized?

❑ Did these early pioneers also found the community? If so, when did they do this? If not, who *were* the founders?

Additional Questions

❑ What was the original name given to the community? Does it have any special significance or meaning?

❑ Are there discernible designs or symbols embedded in the original plan or layout in the community? If so, do these have any special significance? Did Freemasons lay any of the cornerstones?

❑ Were any known curses placed by the original inhabitants on either the land or the people who came after them?

CONFLUENT FACTORS AND EVENTS

❑ What external forces or events have significantly impacted the life and character of the community (e.g., invasions, natural disasters, migrations)?

❑ Was a new language or culture ever imposed on the community as a whole? Did it stick? Did certain socio-economic stratas or ethnic groups adapt to the changes better than others? Why?

❑ If the community's original heritage was godly, when did alternative religions or influences first enter the city in substantial measure?

❑ Did long-term immigrants and/or invaders maintain devotional links to the religious/philosophical systems of their birth nations?

❏ What particular events, coincidences or connections most clearly suggest a demonic master plan at work in the history of the community?

Additional Questions

❏ Have there ever been significant or sudden changes in the economic life of the community (i.e., through famine, technological discontinuity or natural disaster)?

CONSENSUS FACTORS AND EVENTS

❏ What significant decisions have been reached through elections, council meetings or other forms of public decision making? How have these affected the spiritual life and character of the community?
❏ Has slavery or indentured service ever been a part of the area's history?
❏ Have community leaders broken treaties, contracts or covenants?
❏ What adaptive deceptions have played a role in maintaining spiritual bondage within the community (e.g., folk Islam, Christian syncretism)?

THE POTENTIAL FOR SPIRITUAL BREAKTHROUGHS

POSITIONING FOR ACTION

❏ Is the Church in the community desperate for revival? Have there been any public expressions of this sentiment?

❑ Is the Church knowledgeable about the true condition of the community? (Is there, for example, an awareness of the facts and challenges you have uncovered in your research?)

❑ Has there been a measurable increase in the number of focused and committed intercessors within the community?

❑ Are there leaders whose commitment to the land/community is such that they are willing to persevere against any opposition to realize spiritual breakthroughs?

❑ Have churches and denominations begun to drop the barriers to true Christian unity? What are the specific evidences of this?

❑ Has social reconciliation occurred within the larger body of Christ?

❑ Are there any large-scale united prayer efforts within the community (e.g., all-night prayer vigils, neighborhood prayerwalks)? Do these reflect a renewed concern for the lost?

❑ Have spiritual mapping campaigns been launched to focus and sustain united prayer efforts?

❑ Have there been any reconciliation initiatives between the Church and the community? If so, have these borne fruit? How?

❑ Is there a sense of hopeful expectancy among the ranks of the believers?

Additional Questions

❑ Is there any evidence that church financial policies have begun to reflect a new set of ministry priorities?

❑ Is spiritual warfare taken seriously by leading pastors in the community?

❏ Have new cooperative outreach programs begun? Are they bearing any fruit?

RECENT DIVINE INITIATIVES

❏ Has God lifted the prayer burden off faithful intercessors?

❏ Has God revealed specific action plans to Christian leaders?

❏ Has the Church taken bold action in response to these revealed instructions?

❏ Have there been any public power encounters or reported outbreaks of divine signs and wonders? Have these been confirmed?

❏ Have any key figures in the community been converted?

❏ Is there any evidence that large-scale church growth has begun throughout the community?

❏ Have community leaders (political or spiritual) formally renounced historic ties to the spirit world?

❏ Have there been any dramatic political or social wind shifts?

❏ Are there any indications of economic or other forms of judgment?

❏ Has the secular news media talked about divine activity or changing attitudes/values/allegiances within the community?

COMMUNITY ASSESSMENT SCALE

Stage	Description
SBH-1	Recognition of manifest bondage
SBH-2	Initial prayer for revival appetite within local Body of Christ
SBH-3	Emergence of intercessory prayer core
SBH-4	Initial backlash (typically involving attacks on intercessors and their families)
SBH-5	Emergence of persevering leadership with commitment to the land/community
SBH-6	External crises and/or internal conviction lead to a wider recognition of prevailing bondages
SBH-7	Pastoral unity develops through humility/repentance
SBH-8	Social reconciliation occurs within the larger Body of Christ
SBH-9	Preliminary spiritual mapping provides additional details on prevailing bondages within the community
SBH-10	Large-scale united prayer begins
SBH-11	Full-scale spiritual mapping reveals root pacts/bondages and sustains fervent prayer
SBH-12	Secondary backlash (typically involving attacks on key leaders)
SBH-13	Leaders publicly renew commitment to land/community
SBH-14	Strategic neighborhood prayerwalking takes place
SBH-15	Reconciliation occurs between the church and community

SBH=Spiritual Beachhead   SBK=Spiritual Breakthrough   STR=Spiritual Transformation

(Scale continued on following pages)

Stage	Description
SBK-1	Prayer burden lifts
SBK-2	Divine action plan(s) revealed
SBK-3	Christians take bold action in response to divine revelation/instructions
SBK-4	Special developments occur (such as public power encounters or key conversions)
SBK-5	Tertiary backlash (typically involving attacks on entire congregations and ministries)
SBK-6	Christian community rallies through intense spiritual warfare
SBK-7	Large-scale conversions take place
SBK-8	Church growth and systematic discipleship occurs throughout the community

Stage	Description
STR-1	Converted political and spiritual leaders formally renounce historic ties to the spirit world
STR-2	Socio-political renewal sweeps the community
STR-3	Community transformation and divine miracles are acknowledged by the secular news media
STR-4	The community begins to export spiritual light to other places
STR-5	Believers maintain their victory through devotion to fellowship, prayer and God's Word

SBH=Spiritual Beachhead   **SBK=Spiritual Breakthrough**   **STR=Spiritual Transformation**

Notes

1. This chart was derived through careful analysis of more than a dozen transformed communities around the world.
2. Although the developments listed on this chart represent a typical sequence of events, individual experiences may differ.
3. Persevering leadership and united prayer were present in every transformed community case study we looked at.
4. Other common factors were public power encounters; social reconciliation; and diagnostic research (spiritual mapping).
5. The Bible offers several examples of leaders who attracted divine favor through intentional action (e.g. Josiah, Ezra).

SPIRITUAL MAPPING AND COMMUNITY TRANSFORMATION

A GLOSSARY OF RELATED TERMS

Adaptive Deceptions—Deceptive schemes adopted by the enemy to replace earlier strategies whose beguiling powers have waned. These new deceptions may be viewed either as necessary course corrections or as upgrades to the adversary's product line.

Animism—The belief that all natural elements—such as mountains, rivers, trees, thunder, fire, stars, animals and human beings—are endowed with, and linked to, a persuasive and conscious spiritual force.

Archival Unit—A spiritual mapping team cell comprised of individuals skilled in culling information from secondary sources. An archival unit will typically devote significant time to research in libraries and community archives.

Binding the Strongman—Neutralizing the deceptive hold or enchantment that demonic powers have achieved over given human subjects so that the latter can process truth at a heart level.

Character Mapping—The process of identifying, or re-identifying, a community on the basis of its spiritual allegiance, social reputation, and ongoing pattern of behavior. Resulting maps present cities and neighborhoods with new descriptive names and more meaningful boundaries. (Biblical examples include Babylon as "The Mother of Harlots and Nineveh as "the Mistress of Sorceries.")

Character Snapshots—Reassessments of a community's spiritual status in the aftermath of important historical decisions and/or events.

City Gate—Centers of political influence and authority, or portals through which new or important influences enter a community.

City Islands—Communities whose spiritual or philosophical connections are with cultures outside their immediate geographic area. Expanding global networks and large-scale migrations have made these situations more common than ever.

Commitment to the Land—The proposition that single-minded devotion to a particular community necessarily precedes the release of spiritual insight into that community.

Community Transformation—A condition of dramatic sociopolitical renewal that results from God's people entering into corporate vision, corporate repentance and corporate prayer. During these extraordinary seasons the kingdom of God pervades virtually every institution of human endeavor. Confirmation of this new heavenly order is typically provided through the secular media.

Conditions of Pain—Social suffering inflicted by outside parties or circumstances. Common examples include injustice, poverty, violence and disease.

Confluent Events—External influences that flow into the life of a community and help shape its character. These tributaries can include wars, migrations, natural disasters or new state laws. They can also include the arrival of the gospel or a competing ideology.

Contextual Factors—Transformative measures commended by God on the basis of a community's history, habits and ideology. Prime examples include social reconciliation, public miracles, and diagnostic research (spiritual mapping).

Contouring Events—Community choices and/or actions that alter the historical landscape like a river sliding within its banks wears a groove in the earth. These events can include local elections, moral choices (such as the decision to receive or reject the gospel) or actions taken to preserve a deceptive tradition

Core Factors—Two elements—persevering leadership and fervent, united prayer—that appear to initiate divine involvement in the process of community transformation.

Corporate Sin—Group rebellion against God's law and purposes that typically results in corollary injury to a particular person or group. The offending collective may be a family, clan, tribe, neighborhood, city, nation or church.

Corporate Vision—A situation where local ministries subordinate or abandon personal agendas in order to participate in a citywide collective cause.

Data Overlays—Information display sets that are superimposed on city base maps for the purpose of analysis.

Data Sets—A grouping of related information. Data sets represent a specific part of, or perspective on, a larger problem or entity. In spiritual mapping research, useful data sets may include such things as community crime statistics and/or spiritual quest sites.

Discovery Questions—An initial set of questions used by spiritual mapping teams to focus their research. These questions are subdivided under headings related to the status of Christianity, prevailing social bondages, worldviews and allegiances, spiritual opposition, the evolution of current circumstances and the potential for spiritual breakthroughs.

Essential Elements—A term used by the intelligence community when referring to the core of a given research assignment. For field workers, essential elements represent those informational gems that must be fetched for their mission to be considered a success.

Excluded Middle—A term deriving from the observation that the worldview of most non-Westerners is three-tiered: (1) the cosmic, transcendent world on the top, (2) a middle layer featuring supernatural forces on earth and (3) the empirical world of our senses resting comfortably on the bottom. The unique tendency of western society has been to ignore the reality of the middle zone.

Field Unit—A spiritual mapping team cell that extracts useful information from primary research sources within a community. A mobile unit will typically gather this information via observation and interviews.

Geomancy—An ancient system of philosophy and divination that seeks to harmonize human activity with natural patterns. It integrates themes such as ecology, dowsing, architecture, astronomy, astrology, mythology and cosmology. (See also Ley Lines.)

Grid Mapping—The systematic identification of relevant locations, usually spiritual quest sites and social bondage sites, within a given community.

Ground-Level Spiritual Warfare—Ministry activity that is associated with individual bondage and/or demonization.

Head Nests—Psychic habitats consisting of neural patterns created through sinful choices (these can take the form of myths, memes or habits). It is from these potent platforms—the apostle Paul calls them "strongholds"—that deceptive spirits endeavor to manipulate our inner world.

High Places—Specific locations where a community or its leaders pay obeisance to tutelary deities and/or idolatrous philosophies. In Biblical contexts, the term is applied to literal mountains or towers that were elevated over the surrounding terrain.

Identificational Repentance—A two-stage intercessory action that involves: (1) an acknowledgment that one's affinity group (clan, city, nation or organization) has been guilty of specific corporate sin before God and man, and (2) a prayerful petition that God will use personal repudiation of this sin as a redemptive beachhead from which to move into the larger community.

Ideological Export Center—A specific location, most commonly a city, that serves as a recognized distribution point for adverse moral, philosophical and spiritual influences.

Information Control Systems—The means employed to store and retrieve project materials. Effective control systems often utilize record-keeping tools such as appointment calendars, memcons, journals, tape logs and computer databases.

Intercessory Prayer—Petitions, entreaties and thanksgivings made on behalf of another. Intercession also involves the act of standing between the object of prayer and spiritual forces. Where God is concerned, the positioning is taken in order to submit requests; in the case of the devil, it is to deflect his attacks.

Intercessory Unit—A spiritual mapping team cell that is dedicated to petitioning God for guidance, favor and protection. Members are expected to carefully record and review specific promptings, warnings, and confirmations that are gleaned in the place of prayer.

Ley Lines—Geographic continuums of spiritual power (some say physical energy) that are established and/or recognized by certain peoples. Depending on the culture in which they are found, ley lines may be viewed either as conduits through which spiritual power is transmitted or as demarcation lines for spiritual authority. Still others equate ley lines with the symbolic alignment observed in Freemasonry or the Asian practice of feng shui. (See also geomancy.)

Mobile Unit—(See Field Unit.)

Neighborhood Reports—A standardized, spiritual mapping product designed to sustain fervent corporate intercession until community transformation becomes a reality. The most common reports feature a specific town or neighborhood, although the definition is flexible enough to encompass school campuses, large companies, military bases, housing estates and Native American reservations. Reports can be produced by a single congregation or by a coalition of ministries. Their contents, organized in six discreet sections, cover themes ranging from prevailing social bondages to the potential for spiritual breakthroughs.

Occult-Level Spiritual Warfare—A term that pertains to inter-cessory confrontations with demonic forces operating through satanism, witchcraft, shamanism, esoteric philosophies (such as Freemasonry and Tibetan Buddhism) and any number of similar occult vehicles.

Participatory Activities—Direct involvement with questionable spiritual rituals or objects, and/or deliberate exposure to "how to" techniques in books dealing with occult subjects. Such things are forbidden to Christians even in the name of research.

Pilgrimages of Repentance—Journeys undertaken with the intent of addressing past sin and subsequent suffering through identificational repentance. These pilgrimages are often public events that retrace the movements of displaced peoples back to a point of origin.

Power Encounter—A visible, practical demonstration that Jesus Christ is more powerful than the spirits, powers or false gods worshiped or feared by the members of a given society or people group.

Power Points (or Places of Power)—Specific natural or man-made locations that are widely regarded as bridges or crossover points to the supernatural world. Such sites are often made numinous by the investments of faith offered over time by large numbers of people.

Prayer Expeditions—Long-distance, trans-territorial prayer-walks along strategically developed routes. Intercession is offered for entire countries and regions.

Prayer Journeys—Intentional prayerwalking in cities other than one's own. Sites often include capitals and ideological export centers

Prayerwalking—The practice of on-site, street-level intercession. Prayers offered by participants are in response to immediate observations and researched targets.

Prayerwalking Profiles—Brief, non-standardized guides that serve as an aid to prayerwalking. Most include at least some treatment of local history, social bondages and spiritual competition. They also present a brief overview of current problems facing the Body of Christ (apathy, persecution or disunity) and a tour itinerary replete with descriptions of relevant sites.

Primary Sources—Uninterpreted information sources such as artifacts, census reports and human subjects of direct interviews.

Principalities and Powers—Demonic agents and structures that exert deceptive control over co-conspiratorial human political kingdoms and systems.

Progressive Revelation—Incremental disclosure of community intelligence that helps to sustain fervent corporate intercession. The psychology is the same as that which pulls readers through a good mystery novel or hobbyists through a challenging puzzle.

Quid Pro Quo **Contract**—An arrangement whereby individuals or communities offer long-term allegiance to spiritual powers in exchange for deliverance from immediate traumatic circumstances.

Redemptive Gift (or Redemptive Purpose)—A distinct characteristic or facet of every city's life and/or history that can be seized upon by God to demonstrate divine blessing and truth.

Regional Reports—A mapping product that enables Christians to discern the spiritual lay of the land in large cities, counties, states or regions. Although similar in structure to neighborhood reports, they are too large for any single ministry to complete and must be cobbled together over time by multi-church partnerships.

Renewing Allegiances—Steps taken by contemporary generations and communities to reaffirm spiritual pacts and practices initiated by their predecessors. In a considerable number of instances these steps are linked to traditions involving specific rituals, festivals and pilgrimages.

Rules of Interpretation—The fundamental principles for determining the accuracy and relevancy of research data. Important guidelines include contextual analysis, integrity of the source, level of confirmation and scriptural validation.

Secondary Sources—Information sources such as books, articles and dissertations that are generally interpretive in nature.

Social Bondage Sites—Strongholds of community suffering, destabilizing social values and/or destructive vices. Specific examples might include crack houses, nightclubs, gang hideouts, abortion clinics and porno theaters.

Special Briefings—Research packages designed to alert local churches, ministry teams and prayer groups to issues and circumstances that warrant special attention. Subject matter can deal with disturbing trends (such as the renewal of ancient spiritual practices), chronic problems (such as a lack of church growth in a given neighborhood) or unique circumstances (such as new openness to the gospel brought on by traumatic events).

Spiritual Beachhead—The first stage on the road to community transformation. The process begins when a handful of dedicated intercessors seek to stimulate a renewed hunger for unity, holiness, and prayer—especially among community pastors. It ends when intense groundswells of corporate repentance, social reconciliation and united prayer give birth to spiritual breakthroughs. In many instances these developments are sustained by intelligence acquired through cooperative spiritual mapping campaigns.

Spiritual Breakthrough—The second stage on the road to community transformation, breakthroughs are characterized by rapid and substantial church growth. Fueled by fervent, focused prayer, genuine evangelistic breakthroughs tend to spread spontaneously across geographic, ethnic and denominational boundaries.

Spiritual Maintenance—The actions taken by liberated communities to preserve hard-won victories. First and foremost, this means continuing to champion the attitudes and actions (such as unity, prayer, humility and holiness) that attract God's presence. For born-again politicians, journalists, businessmen and educators, it also means perpetuating Kingdom values through the institutions they serve.

Spiritual Mapping—The discipline of diagnosing the obstacles to revival in a given community. Through fervent prayer and diligent research, practitioners are able to measure the landscape of the spiritual dimension and discern moral gateways between it and the material world.

Spiritual Quest Sites—Any natural or man-made location that facilitates spiritual investigation, ritual or worship. Examples include everything from temples and mosques to sacred mountains and metaphysical bookstores.

Spiritual Strongholds—Ideological fortresses that exist both in the human mind and in objective territorial locations. Manifesting both defensive and offensive characteristics, these strongholds simultaneously repel light and export darkness.

Spiritual Territoriality—A concept acknowledging that spiritual powers routinely forge strategies that are uniquely linked to specific cultures and geography. (A clear example of this may be seen in the dissimilar deceptive means employed by the Enemy in the cities of Mecca and Hollywood.)

Spiritual Transformation—(See Community Transformation.)

Spiritual Warfare—Conflicts with demonic strongholds and moral deception that require non-carnal weaponry and spiritual armor (see Eph. 6).

Strategic-Level Spiritual Warfare—A term that pertains to intercessory confrontations with demonic power concentrated over given cities, cultures and peoples.

Suprastate—An area of expanded size and common features or interests (examples include the Navajo Nation, the Arabian Peninsula and the Andean Altiplano). Viewing a community in context helps to identify broader historic and cultural realities that make up a region's spiritual bedrock.

Territorial Spirits—Demonic powers that have been given controlling influence over specific sites, peoples and areas. The belief in such hierarchical arrangements is culturally widespread and often involves protective deities linked to homes, temples, clans, cities, valleys and nations.

Thematic Chronologies—Custom timelines that help track

such things as community responses to trauma or adaptive deceptions that have sustained dynasties of spiritual darkness. These potent devices act like special filters that permit users to take an uncluttered or focused look at the forces at work in their area.

Three Battlegrounds—A term referring to the three primary arenas of spiritual warfare—the mind, the church and the heavenly places. (The term has also been employed in reference to the mind, the heart and the mouth).

Timelines—devices that allow researchers to register important events or milestones. Properly developed, timelines reveal how various influences are woven together to form distinct cultures and communities. They highlight the continuum that links the past to the present and demonstrate how the attitudes and actions of previous generations can have a profound effect on the present day.

Tour Questions—Questions that are designed to encourage respondents to provide an interviewer with full descriptions of particular places or experiences.

Tradition Bearers—A term developed by folklife scholars to describe individuals whose good memories, unique roles, performance skills and/or long lives make them especially well qualified to provide information about a given community.

United Prayer—United prayer is a declaration to the heavenlies that a community of believers is prepared for divine partnership. When this welcoming intercession is joined by knowledge, it becomes focused—leading to and sustaining the kind of fervent prayer that produces results.

Warfare Prayer—The application of strategic-level spiritual warfare to evangelistic efforts. An uprooting of prevailing spiritual strongholds that hinder the gospel.

World Rulers of Darkness—Demonic forces involved in deceptive and destructive manipulation of natural elements and systems.

Worldview—A philosophical paradigm. The perspective adopted by a given individual or culture on the world which surrounds them.

FURTHER RESOURCES

The following resource list includes a collection of organizations, individuals and books that offer practical help to spiritual mappers and churches interested in community transformation. These are "customer service" options, and if you take advantage of them you will save yourself plenty of time and grief.

HELPFUL ORGANIZATIONS

The Sentinel Group
P. O. Box 6334
Lynnwood, WA 98036
Phone: (425) 672-2989   Fax: (425) 672-3028   Toll Free
Orders: (877) 672-2989
E-mail: SentinelGp@aol.com
Web: www.SentinelGroup.org

The Sentinel Group offers perhaps the largest assortment of resources for those interested in spiritual mapping and community transformation. These include live regional seminars, a dedicated electronic mailing list called *The Mapper's Forum*, a dramatic video documentary on transformed communities called *Transformations*, and a variety of training videos, books, tapes, and transparencies.

Others will want to take advantage of the ministry's project review service. For a modest fee (about $15) experienced staff members will evaluate your interim or "completed" research report and draw attention to issues that may have been overlooked. Sentinel will then use these reports (with permission) to create national and continental assessments.

The Sentinel Group also coordinates international spiritual mapping activities through the *Ancient Paths Project*, a large-scale effort aimed at identifying and repudiating early altars and spiritual pacts. If you are interested in obtaining more information on this initiative use the contact numbers listed above.

CitiReach International

5775 N. Union Blvd.

Colorado Springs, CO 80918

Phone: (719) 548-7460   Fax: (719) 548-7475

E-mail: JDennison@compuserve.com

Jack Dennison leads this spinoff of DAWN Ministries. Primarily a consulting agency, CitiReach expects to deploy up to twenty full-time consultants by January 2003. These trained individuals will systematically walk U.S.-based churches through the process of city taking.

Frontline Ministries

P. O. Box 786

Corvallis, OR 97339-0786

Phone: (541) 754-1345   Fax: (541) 754-4140

E-mail: 103112.3123@compuserve.com

Tom White, Frontline's principal consultant, provides outstanding seminars on strategic spiritual warfare, intercession, and prayer evangelism. He works closely with CitiReach International and International Renewal Ministries.

Generals of Intercession
P. O. Box 49788
Colorado Springs, CO 80949
Phone: (719) 535-0977   Fax: (719) 535-0884
E-mail: GENINT@aol.com

Mike and Cindy Jacobs are available to provide training and networking help for churches and prayer teams interested in spiritual mapping and community transformation. Their Colorado Springs office also serves as the headquarters for the U.S. Spiritual Warfare Network.

Harvest Evangelism, Inc.
6155 Almaden Expressway, Suite 400
San Jose, CA 95120
Phone: (408) 927-9052   Fax: (408) 927-9830
E-mail: harvevan@aol.com   Web: www.harvestevan.org

Ed Silvoso and his team are actively engaged in helping churches reach out to their communities through prayer evangelism. Their services range from training seminars and materials to active consulting.

Hispanic International Ministries
P. O. Box 25472
Colorado Springs, CO 80918
Phone: (719) 262-9922   Fax: (719) 260-7277
E-mail: 74114.2104@compuserve.com

Hector Torres is one of the most experienced spiritual mappers in Latin America. In addition to authoring several books on spiritual mapping and community transformation, he is an active seminar speaker and project consultant.

Interdev
P. O. Box 3883
Seattle, WA 98124
Phone: (425) 775-8330   Fax: (425) 775-8326
E-mail: interdev-us@xc.org   interdev-uk@xc.org

Interdev, a Seattle-based ministry headed by Phill Butler, special-izes in teaching Christian organizations how to form and sustain successful partnerships. Services include a range of training options as well as practical consulting.

Mission America
5666 Lincoln Drive
Edina, Mike Nave 55436
Phone: (612) 912-0001   Fax: (612) 912-0002
E-mail: missionamerica@compuserve.com

Mission America is a broad-based ministry consortium offer-ing a wide variety of training, networking and consulting servic-es. Under the leadership of Dr. Paul Cedar the organization has taken an active interest in city reaching and community transfor-mation.

World Prayer Center
P. O. Box 63060
Colorado Springs, CO 80962
Phone: (719) 536-9100
E-mail: info@wpccs.org   Web: www.wpccs.org

The Colorado Springs-based World Prayer Center directed by Peter and Doris Wagner and Chuck Pierce offers a special research library and useful computer databases. It is also home to the Wagner Institute which provides a widerange of training options.

INTERNATIONAL CONTACTS

Victor Lorenzo
Agaces 274/84
1437 Buenos Aires
ARGENTINA
Fax: 54-21-52-9615

Neuza Itioka
Agape Reconciliation
Caixa Postal 2029 CEP
01060-970
São Paulo, SP
BRAZIL
Phone: 011-523-2544   Fax: 011-523-2201
E-mail: neuza97@ibm.net

Alistair Petrie/Helen Thornton
Joshua Connection/Sentinel Ministries
4888 First Avenue
Delta, BC
CANADA, V4 1B3
Phone: 604-943-6572   Fax: 604-943-6532
E-mail: joshconn@bc.sympatico.ca

Randy & Marcy MacMillan
Mission Sur America
Apartados, Aereos 25-500
Cali
COLOMBIA, SA
Phone: 011-572-332-0099   Fax: 011-572-556-0063
E-mail: rmacmillan@telesat.com.co
www.telesat.com.co/comunife

Francesca Fleming
P. O. Box 11905
Harlesden, London, NW10 4RH
ENGLAND
Phone: 0181-357-0233
E-mail: gateway@dircon.oo.uk

Harold Caballeros
El Shaddai Ministries
Section 98, P.O. Box 02-5289
Miami, FL 33102-5289
Phone: 011-502-337-4777   Fax: 011-502-337-0316
E-Mail: Shaddai@ns.guate.net

Raju Abraham
Emmanuel Hospital Association
808/92, Nehru Place
New Delhi, 110 019
INDIA
E-Mail: 106347.3175@compuserve.com

Nozumu Takimoto/Doria Ransom
Strategic Intercession & Research Network
39-10 Higashichoda Hirai Shinshiro
Shi Aichi Ken
441-1361 JAPAN
Phone: 81-5362-3-4547   Fax: 81-5362-3-6786
E-Mail: Nozoshi@quartz.ocn.ne.jp

Thomas Muthee
Word of Faith Church
P. O. Box 1039
Kiambu
KENYA
Phone: 254-154-20158   Fax: 254-2-21-6692

Dexter Low
Gerega Latter Rain Malaysia
2, Jalan 12/3
46200 Petaling Jaya, Selangor
MALAYSIA
Phone: 603-7555345   Fax: 603-7551270

Emeka Nwankpa
P. O. Box 4930, 28 Faulks Road
ABA
NIGERIA
Phone: 46-19-24-70-00   Fax: 46-19-24-70-01
E-Mail: emekan@aol.com

Gerda Leithgöb/Elizabeth Jordaan
Herald Ministry
P. O. Box 72163
Lynnwood Ridge
0040 Pretoria
REPUBLIC of SOUTH AFRICA
Phone: 27-12-348-8312   Fax: 27-12-348-1377
E-Mail: Herald@mweb.com.za

Dominick Yeo
Trinity Christian Centre
Farrer Road
P. O. Box 90
SINGAPORE 912803
Phone: 65-468-4444   Fax: 65-467-6005
E-Mail: tccnet@trinity.org.sg   www.trinity.net

Bob Beckett
The Dwelling Place
27100 Girard
Hemet, CA 92544
UNITED STATES
Phone: 909-658-0717   Fax: 909-766-1080
E-Mail: dwelling@bigfoot.com

John Robb
800 West Chestnut
Monrovia, CA 91016
UNITED STATES
Phone: (626) 301-7713   Fax: (626) 301-7786
E-mail: john_robb@wvi.org

RECOMMENDED READING

Beckett, Bob; Wagner-Sytsema, Rebecca. *Commitment to Conquer.* Grand Rapids: Chosen, 1997.

Dawson, John. *Taking Our Cities for God.* Lake Mary, FL: Creation House, 1989.

Hawthorne, Steve, and Kendrick, Graham. *PrayerWalking: Praying On Site with Insight.* Lake Mary, FL: Creation House, 1993.

Otis, Jr., George. *The Last of the Giants.* Grand Rapids: Chosen, 1991.

—— *The Twilight Labyrinth.* Grand Rapids: Chosen, 1997.

Silvoso, Ed. *That None Should Perish.* Ventura, CA: Regal, 1994.

Torres, Hector. *Comunidades Transformadas por la Oracion.* Nashville, TN: Betania, 1999.

Wagner, Peter C. ed. *Breaking Strongholds in Your City.* Ventura, CA: Regal, 1993.

—— *Praying with Power.* Ventura, CA: Regal, 1997.

White, Tom. *Breaking Strongholds: How Spiritual Warfare Sets Captives Free.* Ann Arbor, MI: Vine Books, 1993.